W9-AGK-478

THINKING
FOR A
CHANGE

THINKING
FOR A
CHANGE

11 WAYS HIGHLY SUCCESSFUL PEOPLE
APPROACH LIFE and WORK

JOHN C. MAXWELL

NEW YORK   BOSTON

If you purchase this book without a cover you should be aware that this book may have been stolen property and reported as "unsold and destroyed" to the publisher. In such case neither the author nor the publisher has received any payment for this "stripped book."

© 2002 by John C. Maxwell

All rights reserved. No part of this book may be reproduced in any form or by any electronic or mechanical means, including information storage and retrieval systems, without permission in writing from the publisher, except by a reviewer who may quote brief passages in a review.

Scriptures noted NIV are taken from the HOLY BIBLE: NEW INTERNATIONAL VERSION®. Copyright © 1973, 1978, 1984, by International Bible Society. Used by permission of Zondervan Publishing House. All rights reserved.

Scriptures noted NRSV are taken from the NEW REVISED STANDARD VERSION of the Bible. Copyright © 1989 by the Division of Christian Education of the National Council of The Churches of Christ in the U.S.A. All rights reserved.

The author is represented by Yates & Yates, LLP, Literary Agency, Orange, California.

Warner Business Books
Warner Books

Time Warner Book Group
1271 Avenue of the Americas, New York, NY 10020
Visit our Web site at www.twbookmark.com.

The Warner Business Books logo is a trademark of Warner Books.

Printed in the United States of America
First Warner Books Printing: March 2003
Special Sales Edition: February 2004
10 9 8 7 6 5 4 3 2 1

The Library of Congress has cataloged the hadcover edition as follows:

Maxwell, John C., 1947–
    Thinking for a change : 11 ways highly successful approach life and work /
John Maxwell.
        p.   cm.
    ISBN 0-446-52957-5
    1. Success in business. 2. Creative thinking. 3. Attitude change. I. Title.
    HF5386.M445   2003
    650.1—dc21

                                                    20002038016

    ISBN 0-446-69393-6 (Special Sales Edition)

Book design by Giorgetta Bell McRee
Cover design by Brand Navigation

This book is dedicated to . . .

All the good thinkers who have shared their thinking
with me over the years.
Thank you for your investment in me.

ACKNOWLEDGMENTS

I'd like to say thank you to
Margaret Maxwell, who shares her thinking with me daily
Charlie Wetzel, who does my writing
Kathie Wheat, who does my research
Stephanie Wetzel, who proofs and edits each chapter
Linda Eggers, who runs my life
and the people who shared their ideas for this book:
Dick Biggs
Kevin Donaldson
Tim Elmore
John Hull
Gabe Lyons
Larry Maxwell
Kevin Myers
Dan Reiland
Kevin Small
J. L. Smith
Dave Sutherland
Rolf Zettersten

CONTENTS

Contents

FORETHOUGHT:
THE DIFFERENCE THAT REALLY
MAKES A DIFFERENCE

Why are some people successful and others not? That question has been asked millions of times. You'll hear many answers. Consider some of the popular ones:

- Successful people get better opportunities.
- People who do not succeed have bad backgrounds.
- Education makes all the difference.
- Failure results from bad breaks.
- Some people are smart; others aren't.
- Lazy people don't succeed.

I've looked for answers to that question throughout my life. Let me tell you a story that I believe reveals the solution.

A friend of mine has two daughters. Kim, the 21-year-old younger daughter, applied to pharmacy school during her senior year of college. On the day she got word of her acceptance, her older sister, Jennie, who is 25, was there to share the news. Kim was ecstatic. Jennie felt glad that Kim had achieved her goal, but she also pitied her.

"Mom," she said, "I feel sorry for Kim. She is going to have to go to school for four more years!"

One daughter thinks: "I have just earned an opportunity for

a future career." Her sister thinks: "She has to go to school for four more years!"

Here's the difference:

Successful people think differently than unsuccessful people.

One sister heard the news and felt excited because she thought about the lucrative, rewarding career about to open up to her. The other sister thought only about the amount of time it would take to achieve it.

How skilled is your thinking? Does your thinking help you achieve? This book identifies eleven types of thinking that successful people employ. Which type of thinking do you believe will increase your odds for success?

Small Thinking or Big-Picture Thinking?
Scattered Thinking or Focused Thinking?
Restrictive Thinking or Creative Thinking?
Fantasy Thinking or Realistic Thinking?
Random Thinking or Strategic Thinking?
Limited Thinking or Possibility Thinking?
Impulsive Thinking or Reflective Thinking?
Popular Thinking or Innovative Thinking?
Solo Thinking or Shared Thinking?
Selfish Thinking or Unselfish Thinking?
Wishful Thinking or Bottom-Line Thinking?

If you're currently not successful, or you are not as successful as you would like to be, it may be because you are not *thinking* your way to the top. To place yourself on the pathway of success, I suggest that you do the following:

Forethought

- Read each chapter to better understand successful thinking.
- Evaluate yourself at the end of each chapter by answering the thinking question.
- Take the action steps included to implement the kind of successful thinking described in the chapter.

Together for the next fourteen chapters, we will take a thinking trip. It could be the difference that makes all the difference in your life!

THOUGHTS ABOUT THINKING

1. **Everything begins with a thought.**
   "Life consists of what a man is thinking about all day."
   —RALPH WALDO EMERSON

2. **What we think determines who we are. Who we are determines what we do.**
   "The actions of men are the best interpreters of their thoughts."
   —JOHN LOCKE

3. **Our thoughts determine our destiny. Our destiny determines our legacy.**
   "You are today where your thoughts have brought you.
   You will be tomorrow where your thoughts take you."
   —JAMES ALLEN

4. **People who go to the top think differently than others.**
   "Nothing limits achievement like small thinking; Nothing expands possibilities like unleashed thinking."
   —WILLIAM ARTHUR WARD

5. **We *can* change the way we think.**
   "Whatever things are true . . . noble . . . just . . . pure . . . lovely . . . are of good report, if there is any virtue and if there is anything praiseworthy; think on these things."
   —PAUL THE APOSTLE

PART I

CHANGE YOUR THINKING
AND CHANGE YOUR LIFE

Chapter 1
Understand the Value of Good Thinking

*"Nurture great thoughts, for you will never
go higher than your thoughts."*
—BENJAMIN DISRAELI

What Were They Thinking?

"Things are more like they are now than they ever were before."
—DWIGHT D. EISENHOWER,
thirty-fourth president of the United States

What one thing do all successful people have in common? What one thing separates those who go to the top from those who never seem to get there? The answer: **Good Thinking!** Those who embrace good thinking as a lifestyle understand the relationship between their level of thinking and their level of progress. They also realize that to change their lives, they must change their thinking.

A DIFFERENT WAY TO THINK

I've been a student of good thinking all my life, so I know how important it is for making progress. In the first book I wrote back in 1979, titled *Think on These Things*, I said, "Your life today is a result of your thinking yesterday. Your life tomorrow will be determined by what you think today."[1] The title of that book was inspired by the words of the Apostle Paul, who admonished us,

> Whatever is true, whatever is honorable, whatever is just, whatever is pure, whatever is pleasing, whatever is commendable, if there is any excellence and if there is anything worthy of praise, think about these things.[2]

My father, Melvin Maxwell, often quoted those words to me. He felt they were important. Why? Because he is an example of someone who changed his life as a result of changing his thinking.

If you met my dad, he would tell you that he was born with a naturally negative bent to his thinking. In addition, he grew up during the Depression, and when he was six years old, his mother died. He was not a happy or hopeful child. But as a teenager, he began to see that all the successful people he knew had one thing in common: they filled their lives with positive thoughts about themselves and others. He desired to be successful like them, so he embarked on the daily task of changing his thinking. To his delight, after much time and effort, his thinking changed him.

People who know him today see Dad as a totally positive person. They would be surprised to find out that he started his life with a negative mind-set. This change in his thinking allowed him to rise to a level of living that seemed above his potential. He went on to be the most successful person in his professional circle. He became a college president and touched the lives of innumerable people. To this day he is my hero.

Changing from negative to positive thinking isn't always

easy, especially if you have a difficult time with change. For some, it's a life-long struggle. Do you know what most people's number one challenge is when it comes to making positive personal changes? It's their feelings. They want to change, but they don't know how to get past their emotions. But there is a way to do it. Take a look at the truth contained in the following syllogism:

Major Premise: I can control my thoughts.
Minor Premise: My feelings come from my thoughts.
Conclusion: I can control my feelings by controlling my
    thoughts.

If you are willing to change your thinking, you can change your feelings. If you change your feelings, you can change your actions. And changing your actions—based on good thinking—can change your life.

WHO WILL CHANGE YOUR MIND?

Most people in our culture look to educational systems to teach them and their children to think. In fact, many individuals believe that formal education holds the key to improving lives and reforming society. James Bryant Conant, chemistry professor and former president of Harvard University, asserted, "Public education is a great instrument of social change. . . . Education is a social process, perhaps the most important process in determining the future of our country, it should command a far larger portion of our national income than it does today."

Many educators would have us believe that good grades lead to a better life, and that the more formal education you have, the more successful you will be. Yet education often can't deliver on such promises. Don't you know highly educated people who are highly unsuccessful? Haven't you met college professors with Ph.D.s who cannot manage their lives effectively? And conversely, don't you know of dropouts who have become very successful? (Think of Bill Gates, Thomas Edison, Federico Fellini, Steve Jobs.)

William Feather, author of *The Business of Life*, remarked, "Two delusions fostered by higher education are that what is taught corresponds to what is learned, and that it will somehow pay off in money." Educational reformer and former University of Chicago president Robert M. Hutchins observed, "When we listen to the radio, look at television and read the newspapers we wonder whether universal education has been the great boon that its supporters have always claimed it would be." Perhaps we would be better off if we took the advice of Mark Twain, who said, "I never let my schooling interfere with my education."

The problem with most educational institutions is that they try to teach people *what* to think, not *how* to think. Contrary to what Francis Bacon said, knowledge alone is not power. Knowledge has value only in the hands of someone who has the ability to think well. People must learn *how* to think well to achieve their dreams and to reach their potential.

WHY YOU SHOULD EMBRACE THE VALUE OF GOOD THINKING

Georgia State University professor David J. Schwartz says, "Where success is concerned, people are not measured in inches or pounds or college degrees or family background; they are measured by the size of their thinking."[3] Becoming a better thinker is worth your effort because the way you think really impacts every aspect of your life. It doesn't matter whether you are a businessperson, teacher, parent, scientist, pastor, or corporate executive. Good thinking *will* improve your life. It will help you to become an achiever. It will make you a *better* businessperson, teacher, parent, scientist, pastor, or executive.

Take a look at just a few reasons why good thinking is so important:

1. Good Thinking Creates the Foundation for Good Results

In *As a Man Thinketh*, James Allen, philosopher of the human spirit, wrote, "Good thoughts and actions can never produce bad results; bad thoughts and actions can never produce good results. This is but saying that nothing can come from corn but corn, nothing from nettles but nettles. Men understand this law in the natural world, and work with it; but few understand it in the mental and moral world (though its operation there is just as simple and undeviating), and they, therefore, do not cooperate with it.[4]

> "Good thoughts and actions can never produce bad results; bad thoughts and actions can never produce good results."
> —James Allen

It may seem obvious that the quality of people's thinking leads to the quality of their results. I believe most people would agree that:

- Poor thinking produces negative progress.
- Average thinking produces no progress.
- Good thinking produces some progress.
- Great thinking produces great progress.

Yet, one of the reasons people don't achieve their dreams is that they desire to change their results without changing their thinking. But that's never going to work. If you expect to reap corn when you planted nettles, you're not going to get corn— no matter how much time you spend watering, fertilizing, or cultivating your plants. If you don't like the crop you are reaping, you need to change the seed you are sowing! Do you want to achieve? Then sow the "seed" of good thinking.

My friend, Bill McCartney, is a three-time Big Eight Conference coach of the year and two-time UPI coach of the year. In 1990, he led the University of Colorado football team to a national championship. He understands what it takes to win in sports. What may surprise many is that he says the mental aspect of the game is more important than the physical. Coach Mac observes, "Mental is to physical what four is to one." No matter how gifted athletes may be physically, if they don't have what it takes mentally, they won't succeed.

> One of the reasons people don't achieve their dreams is that they desire to change their results without changing their thinking.

I was reminded again of that truth at a recent leadership conference. I told the attendees that I was working on a book called *Thinking for a Change*. During one of the breaks, a man named Richard McHugh came up and told me a little about his experience as a competitive bull rider. After the conference, he sent me a letter telling the whole story. He wrote,

Dear Dr. Maxwell:

I discovered the importance of "thinking" my way to success during my career as a bull rider. I started bull riding with the amateur bull-riding circuit. Not long after I moved to the top of the amateur circuit I yearned to join the professional bull riding association, so I looked to the top for a teacher. I met and started a relationship with a world champion bull rider who lived in my area. His name was Gary Leffew.

Gary invited me to his professional bull-riding arena at his ranch. After it became clear to Gary that I had committed myself to a career as a bull rider, he agreed to help me. He told me that the first thing I would have to do is quit the amateur rodeo circuit. Gary said, "As long as you are hanging around amateurs, you will think like an amateur, and you will not improve your skills." That day I went from the top of the amateur bull riders to the bottom of the professionals.

After getting my professional cowboy association permit, I went back to Gary's rodeo arena, and I was ready to get on some bulls. Much to my surprise, Gary met up with me that day, gave me a book, and sent me on my way. The book was *Psycho-Cybernetics* by Maxwell Maltz. Now, you have to understand that for a cowboy, this was a major paradigm shift. All of the other seasoned bull riders were telling me, "If you want to ride bulls, the secret is just getting on as many bulls as your body can withstand in terms of the pain." But they were not World Champion bull riders like my mentor was. So I took Gary's advice instead, and I went home and read the book.

When I finished, I went back to Gary, and I couldn't believe what he did next: he gave me another book on thinking! A few more visits to Gary's ranch netted me more books. I read every one.

Now, some people might think this is crazy, but I yearned to ride a bull. On one visit to Gary's, I finally told him that I had read every book that he gave me, but now I wanted to get on some bulls! Gary explained to me, "Rich, before you ride bulls," and pointed to his head, "you've got to ride BULLS!" [meaning that the process of visualization had to come first}. Now I understood what he was doing: preparing me mentally for riding bulls! "Okay," I told him, "so now that I've read all those books, I'm ready to get on a bull!" I was wrong. The next step, Gary explained, was cassette tapes. Volumes of tapes!

When Gary finally said I was ready to get on a bull, it was a stationary barrel bull! There I learned how to visualize every bull movement and counter movement.

The next lesson I learned was about association. "Who you hang around with," Gary explained, "can influence how you think." As I began traveling in the professional bull riders circuit, I learned that it was important to be with the riders who were winning. My mentor told me that if I couldn't find any winning bull riders to ride with, then I was to travel alone to protect my new winning mental attitude.

Dr. Maxwell, I'd like to tell you that I went on to win the world championship; I didn't. But I did win a lot of rodeos, and I did make a lot of money riding in the professional bull-riding circuit. This cowboy eventually left the rodeo circuit and married a wonderful woman. We now own one of the largest employment agencies on the central coast of California.

I guess I'm still thinking my way to the top.

Sincerely,

Richard McHugh

To make progress in any field, you have to take action. But the success of the action you take depends entirely on how you think beforehand. What Claude M. Bristol wrote in *The Magic of Believing* is true: "The successful people in industry have succeeded through their thinking. Their hands were helpers to their brains."

2. *Good Thinking Increases Your Potential*

Author James Allen believed, "You will become as small as your controlling desire, as great as your dominant aspiration."[5] Or to paraphrase the words of King Solomon, wisest of all ancient kings, "As people think in their hearts, so they are."[6] If your thinking shapes who you are, then it naturally follows that your potential is determined by your thinking.

In *The 21 Irrefutable Laws of Leadership*, I wrote about the Law of the Lid, which states, "Leadership ability determines a person's level of effectiveness." In other words, in any endeavor with people, your leadership is the lid. If you're a poor leader, your lid is low. If you are a great leader, your lid is high. I believe that your thinking has a similar impact on your life. Your thinking is the lid for your potential. If you're an excellent thinker, then you have excellent potential, and the words of Emerson ring

| Progress is often just a good idea away. |

true: "Beware when the great God lets loose a great thinker on the planet." But if your thinking is poor, then you have a lid on your life.

Achieving your potential comes from making progress, and progress is often just one good idea away. That was certainly true of Sam Walton, the founder of Wal-Mart. He explained, "I guess in all my years, what I heard more often than anything was: a town of less than 50,000 in population cannot support a discount store for very long." But Walton did not think the way his competitors thought, and for that reason, his potential was greater. While other merchants followed popular thinking, Walton thought for himself and struck out on his own. That has paid off in a remarkable way. Today Wal-Mart is the world's largest retailer, employing more than one million people and achieving annual sales in excess of $191 billion. Every week more than 100 million customers visit Wal-Mart stores.[7] How's that for potential! No wonder Jack Welch, former chairman of General Electric, said, "The hero is the one with ideas."

> "The hero is the one with ideas."
> —Jack Welch

The greatest detriment to many people's success tomorrow is their thinking today. If their thinking is limited, so is their potential. But if people can keep growing in their thinking, they will constantly outgrow what they're doing. And their potential will always be off the charts.

3. Good Thinking Produces More Good Thinking IF . . . You Make It a Habit

Albert Einstein observed, "The problems we face today cannot be solved on the same level of thinking we were at when we created them." Look around and you'll see that is true. The world keeps getting more and more complicated. Does that discourage you? It doesn't have to. Many years ago, I came across a quote that made a tremendous impression on me. It said,

> I am your constant companion. I am your greatest helper or heaviest burden. I will push you onward or drag you down to failure. I am completely at your command. Half of the things you do you might just as well turn over to me and I will be able to do them quickly and correctly. I am easily managed—you must merely be firm with me. Show me exactly how you want something done and after a few lessons I will do it automatically.
>
> I am the servant of all great men; and alas, of all failures as well. Those who are great, I have made great. Those who are failures, I have made failures. I am not a machine, though I work with all the precision of a machine plus the

intelligence of a man. You may run me for profit or run me for ruin—it makes no difference to me. Take me, train me, be firm with me, and I will place the world at your feet. Be easy with me and I will destroy you.

Who am I? I am habit![8]

The good news is that no matter how complicated life gets or how difficult problems may seem, good thinking can make a difference—if you make it a consistent part of your life. The more you engage in good thinking, the more good thoughts will come to you. Success comes to those who habitually do things that unsuccessful people don't do. Achievement comes from the habit of good thinking. The more you engage in good thinking, the more good thoughts you will continue to think. It's like creating a neverending army of ideas capable of achieving almost anything. As playwright Victor Hugo asserted, "An invasion of armies can be resisted, but not an invasion of ideas."

> "An invasion of armies can be resisted, but not an invasion of ideas."
> —Victor Hugo

Every year, I talk to tens of thousands of people on the subjects of leadership, teamwork, and personal growth. I've found that many of them believe good thinking is so complicated that it lies beyond their reach. But in truth, it's really a very simple process. Every person has the potential to become a good thinker. I've observed that . . .

- Unsuccessful people focus their thinking on survival
- Average people focus their thinking on maintenance
- Successful people focus their thinking on progress

A change of thinking can help you move from survival or maintenance to real progress. Ninety-five percent of achieving anything is knowing what you want and paying the price to get it.

PORTRAIT OF A GOOD THINKER

So how do you pay the price to become a good thinker? For that matter, what does a good thinker look like? You often hear someone say that a colleague or friend is a "good thinker," but that phrase means something different to everyone. To one person it may mean having a high IQ, while to another it could mean knowing a bunch of trivia or being able to figure out whodunit when reading a mystery novel. I believe that good thinking isn't just one thing. It consists of several specific thinking skills. Becoming a good thinker means developing those skills to the best of your ability.

In *Built to Last*, Jim Collins and Jerry Porras describe what it means to be a visionary company, the kind of company that epitomizes the pinnacle of American business. They describe those companies this way:

> A visionary company is like a great work of art. Think of Michelangelo's scenes from Genesis on the ceiling of the Sistine Chapel or his statue of David. Think of a great and enduring novel like *Huckleberry Finn* or *Crime and Punishment*. Think of Beethoven's Ninth Symphony or Shakespeare's *Henry V*. Think of a beautifully designed building, like the masterpieces of Frank Lloyd Wright or Ludwig Mies van der Rohe. You can't point to any one single item that makes the whole thing work; it's the entire work—all the pieces working together to create an overall effect—that leads to enduring greatness.[9]

Good thinking is similar. You need all the thinking "pieces" to become the kind of person who can achieve great things. Those pieces include the following eleven skills:

- Seeing the Wisdom of Big-Picture Thinking
- Unleashing the Potential of Focused Thinking
- Discovering the Joy of Creative Thinking
- Recognizing the Importance of Realistic Thinking
- Releasing the Power of Strategic Thinking
- Feeling the Energy of Possibility Thinking
- Embracing the Lessons of Reflective Thinking
- Questioning the Acceptance of Popular Thinking
- Encouraging the Participation of Shared Thinking
- Experiencing the Satisfaction of Unselfish Thinking
- Enjoying the Return of Bottom-Line Thinking

As you read the chapters dedicated to each kind of thinking, you will discover that *Thinking for a Change* does not try to tell you what to think; it attempts to teach you *how* to think. As you become acquainted with each skill, you will find that some you do well, others you don't. Learn to develop each of those kinds of thinking, and you will become a better thinker. Master all that you can—including the process of shared thinking which helps you compensate for your weak areas—and your life will change.

ADVICE FROM A GOOD THINKER

I once read that "the battle for control and leadership of the world has always been waged most effectively at the idea level. An idea, whether right or wrong, that captures the minds of a nation's youth will soon work its way into every area of society,

especially in our multimedia age. Ideas determine consequences."[10]

I get to see the power of ideas at work in the lives of young
people every day because my company, The INJOY Group,
employs many sharp leaders in their
twenties and thirties. Gabe Lyons, an
INJOY vice president, recently
attended an event at the Fox Theater
in downtown Atlanta and came back
on fire with enthusiasm. The speaker
for the occasion was Jack Welch,
former CEO of General Electric. Gabe went that day because
he is a student of leadership and personal development, and he
wanted to learn from one of the finest business leaders in the
world.

> "The battle for control and leadership of the world has always been waged most effectively at the idea level."
> —The American Covenant

Gabe was one of about six hundred business people in
attendance. Jack Welch came to promote his book, *Jack:
Straight from the Gut*, but he didn't read from the book
or give a canned lecture. He did something much more valuable for his audience: he answered their questions. Gabe said
that for almost two hours, pure gold dripped from Jack's
mouth. The best thing Gabe learned came in response to a
question from a young business person in his mid-twenties.
Gabe says,

A young guy asked, "When you were my age, what did
you do to elevate yourself among all of your other associ-
ates? How did you stand out from the crowd of other
young, ambitious and driven colleagues of your day?"
Jack responded, "Great question, young man. And this is
an important point for every person to hear. The first
thing you must understand is the importance of getting
out of 'the pile.' The only way you are going to stand out

Appointments

Mon _____ _____

Tues _____ _____

Wed _____ _____

Thurs_____ _____

Fri _____ _____

Sat _____ _____

Sun _____ _____

(503) 641-7740

Mike D. Gotesman, L.C.S.W.

Counseling and Hypnotherapy

3800 S.W. Cedar Hills Blvd. Suite 201

Beaverton, Oregon 97005

(503) 641-7740

to your boss is to understand this simple principle: When your boss asks you a question, assigns a basic project, or sends you out to gather some data, you must understand that your boss already knows the answer he is looking for. As a matter of fact, in most cases, he simply wants you to go out and confirm what he already believes is true in his gut.

"Most people simply go out and do just that," Jack continued, "confirm what their boss believed to be true. But here is the difference maker. You must understand that the question is only the beginning. When your boss asks you a question, that question should become the jumping off point for several more ideas and thoughts. If you want to elevate yourself, you must sink your thoughts and time into not only answering the question, but going above and beyond it to add value to the train of thought your boss was on.

"Practically speaking, that means coming back to the table and presenting to your boss not only an answer, but three or more other ideas, options and perspectives that were probably not previously considered by your boss. The goal is to add value to the idea and the thought by exceeding expectations when the question is given to you. This is true not only with questions, but assignments, initiatives and everything else ever given to you to run with by upper management."

Jack drove the point home emphatically. "So if you understand that the question is only the beginning, you will get out of the pile fast, *because 99.9 percent of all employees are in the pile because they don't think.* If you understand this principle, you will always be given more critical questions to answer. And in time, you will be the one giving out the questions to others!"

> "Ninety-nine point nine percent of all employees are in the pile because they don't think."
> —Jack Welch

If you desire to climb up out of the pile, to rise beyond your circumstances, to move up to another level in your career and personal life, then you need to take the advice of Jack Welch. You need to become the best thinker you can be. It can revolutionize your life.

THINKING QUESTION

Do I believe that good thinking can change my life?

Understanding Good Thinking

1. Who are the best thinkers you know? Name them.

_____

_____

2. What separates them from the rest of the crowd? Describe what's different about them.

_____

_____

_____

Choose one of those thinkers and try to arrange to spend some time with him or her. Whom you associate with matters.

3. In the past, how would you have defined good thinking? How would you describe it now?

_____

_____

4. What personal or professional issues have created ongoing obstacles to your progress? Don't try to solve them now. Simply describe them here:

_____

_____

Chapter 2
Realize the Impact of Changed Thinking

"You can't stop people from thinking—but you can start them."
—FRANK A. DUSCH

What Were They Thinking?

"We're going to turn this team around 360 degrees."
—JASON KIDD, upon being drafted into the NBA

It's easy to believe that unsuccessful people need to change their thinking. But how about people who have achieved some degree of success? Can individuals go to the next level without changing the way they think? Karen Ford can answer that question. I met Karen back in 1998 before speaking on leadership to a large group of Mary Kay consultants. That's when she told me her story.

A BEND IN THE ROAD

Karen Ford didn't set out in life to be a businessperson or entrepreneur. She started out as a teacher. "When I graduated from high school, there were very limited choices for women at the time," says Karen. "It was either teaching or nursing, and I went to a teaching college, so I became an elementary teacher." For ten years she taught second grade, and she was good at it.

But in 1987, her circumstances radically changed. Her second child was born with a heart condition that required him to receive medication every four hours, every day, for a year. Since a parent had to administer the medicine, Karen left her job and stayed home to care for her son.

That put her family in a financial bind, so she began looking for a solution. Soon she decided to try Mary Kay. It appealed to her because she could earn $50 a week to make up for her lost teaching income. She made plans to sell cosmetics for a year, and then when her son had recovered, she would return to her career in teaching.

Surprised by Success

That's what Karen expected to happen, but she found that she really enjoyed working with Mary Kay, and that she was good at it—*really* good at it. "I was making more income than I ever thought possible," she says. "I was being awarded diamonds, trips, cars." A new life was opening up to her, and she was discovering gifts and talents that had gone untapped. She never returned to the classroom.

For the next couple of years, Karen worked hard selling products, recruiting like-minded women, and building her own organization. At Mary Kay, each woman is an independent businessperson. The company, which works with more than 750,000 beauty consultants, operates by this philosophy: "In business for yourself but not by yourself." Karen's success soon made her part of an exclusive group: she became one of 8,200 independent sales directors. But she wanted more. She believed she could go to the next level—the highest level in Mary Kay. She wanted to become a national sales director.

For the next five years, Karen worked tirelessly to achieve her goal. She recruited others. She expanded her reach, and she hit one sales objective after another. She increased her sales from an already impressive half a million dollars a year to more than $650,000. She believed she had done everything needed to make it to the highest level. But when the call finally came from Mary Kay in 1995, it was to tell her that she had *not* been appointed a national sales director. The news disappointed her, but even more difficult was the criticism that followed. Karen learned that the main reason she hadn't made it was that she had gathered a bunch of followers who simply were trying to carry out her dreams and goals, not leaders who could achieve on their own and rally others to succeed. "I came to realize that leading leaders was a lot harder than I thought," she recalls. It was Karen's first real failure, and she felt devastated.

CHANGING HER MIND

Karen felt so disheartened that she nearly quit Mary Kay. She seriously considered accepting an offer with another company training leaders, a job that would have required about twelve hours of work each month for a six-figure annual income. Several times she even attempted to write her letter of resignation, but she just couldn't do it. She kept thinking about the people in her organization and their hopes and dreams. She didn't want to change her goal. So instead, she determined to change herself.

"It was a very conscious decision not to quit, but when I made that decision, I knew that I had to change my thinking in order to move forward," says Karen. "The first person I needed to work on and adjust was myself." Since she knew she could not succeed by thinking the way she had, she went on a personal growth binge, devouring every leadership book and tape she could get her hands on. For months, she virtually ignored her organization and did nothing but work on herself and how she thought. She made it her goal to learn how to lead leaders.

When she reemerged and began to work with her colleagues again, she did more than simply cast vision and rely on motivation; instead she put her new thinking skills to use. She looked at everything differently. She started creating strategies and systems that would help her people to grow just as she had. And she determined to become the best businessperson she could at her *current* level. Ironically, that is what took her to the next level.

Novelist Leo Tolstoy observed, "Everyone thinks of changing the world, but no one thinks of changing himself." Because Karen changed herself from the inside out, she began attracting different kinds of individuals— people who could think and lead as she did. And she took them to new levels of achievement. On October 1, 1998, she received another phone call from Mary Kay headquarters.

> "Everyone thinks of changing the world, but no one thinks of changing himself."
> —Leo Tolstoy

This time she was informed that she had accomplished what only 170 other Mary Kay consultants around the world had done. She had been named a national sales director. And it happened only because she had changed her thinking.

WHY YOU SHOULD CHANGE YOUR THINKING

It's hard to overstate the value of changing your thinking. Good thinking can do many things for you: generate revenue, solve problems, and create opportunities. It can take you to a whole new level—personally and professionally. It really can change your life.

Consider some things you need to know about changing your thinking:

1. Changed Thinking Is Not Automatic

As I started working on this book, I talked to a few key people in my life who I know are good thinkers. One of those people is my brother Larry, who gave me this quote: "Neither Laurel nor Hardy had any bad thoughts. Matter of fact, they had no thoughts at all!" If you've seen any of their old movies, you know what he's talking about. Their lack of good thinking was the major source of their comic predicaments.

> "Neither Laurel nor Hardy had any bad thoughts. Matter of fact, they had no thoughts at all."
> —Larry Maxwell

Unfortunately, too many people take after Laurel and Hardy. Sadly, a change in thinking doesn't happen on its own. Good ideas rarely go out and find someone. If you want to find a good idea, you must search for it.

If you want to become a better thinker, you need to work at it—and once you begin to become a better thinker, the good ideas keep coming. In fact, the amount of good thinking you can do at any time depends primarily on the amount of good thinking you are already doing.

2. Changed Thinking Is Difficult

When you hear someone say, "Now this is just off the top of my head," expect dandruff. The only people who believe thinking is easy are those who don't habitually engage in it. Nobel Prize-winning physicist Albert Einstein, one of the best thinkers who ever lived, asserted, "Thinking is hard work; that's why so few do it." Because thinking is so difficult, you want to use anything you can to help you improve the process. (In the next chapter, I offer a strategy for becoming more intentional about your thinking.)

3. Changed Thinking Is Worth the Investment

Author Napoleon Hill observed, "More gold has been mined from the thoughts of man than has ever been taken from the earth." When you take the time to learn how to change your thinking and become a better thinker, you are investing in yourself. Gold mines tap out. Stock markets crash. Real estate investments can go sour. But a human mind with the ability to think well is like a diamond mine that never runs out. It's priceless.

> "More gold has been mined from the thoughts of men than has ever been taken from the earth."
> —Napoleon Hill

4. Changed Thinking Is the Best Gift You Can Give Others

Author H. L. Mencken asserted, "My guess is that well over 80 percent of the human race goes through life without a single original thought." When Karen Ford changed the way she thought, she improved not only her own life, but also the lives of all the people in her organization. Learning to think better is a great investment in yourself—but it's also the greatest present you can give someone else, because it represents the gift of unlimited potential.

The Impact of Changed Thinking

Most people who don't feel content with their lives don't know the reason why. Often they suspect that circumstances or other people are to blame. Even honest and self-aware individuals who know the problem lies inside of them still may have trouble getting to the root of the issue. They ask themselves, "Why am I this way?" They desire to change, but they don't do anything differently so that they *can* change. They merely hope things will turn out all right—and they become frustrated when they don't. Recognize that only when you make the right changes to your thinking do other things begin to turn out right in your life.

Before I outline how changing your thinking changes your life, I need to mention something. One person cannot change another person. For too many years as a motivational teacher, I tried to change people, and it didn't work. I had good intentions, but I finally realized something: I was responsible *to* people but not *for* them. As a leader, I needed to teach the value of changed thinking and how to make those necessary changes; but the people themselves were responsible to make the changes.

> Only when you make the right changes to your thinking do other things begin to turn out right.

In the next few pages, you will see how you can change yourself when you take responsibility to change your thinking. Follow the process faithfully and it will result in a changed life! Here is how it works:

Step 1: Changing Your Thinking Changes Your Beliefs

Karen Ford remarked, "People will never attain what they cannot see themselves doing." When Karen determined to improve herself by learning to be a better thinker, her beliefs changed. She observed, "A belief in my personal abilities is what changed first." That was important. Her initial failure to achieve her dream shook her self-confidence. But once she had gained thinking skills that made it possible for her to lead more effectively, she regained her confidence. And she began to look at others differently. She saw people's potential and made it her goal to teach them to think. The skills they gained helped them to believe in themselves. Without that belief, they could not move forward.

> "People will never attain what they cannot see themselves doing."
> —Karen Ford

My friend author Gordon MacDonald says,

In our pressurized society, people who are out of shape mentally usually fall victim to ideas and systems that are destructive to the human spirit and to human relationships. They are victimized because they have not been taught how to think, nor have they set themselves to the life-long pursuit of the growth of the mind. Not having the facility of a strong mind, they grow dependent upon the thoughts and opinions of others. Rather than deal with ideas and issues, they reduce themselves to lives full of rules, regulations, and programs.

Or they simply give up, as Karen Ford was tempted to do. But here's the good news: even if you currently lack what MacDonald calls "a strong mind," there's no reason to give up or live an unfulfilling life. The human mind *can* change. In fact, that's one of the things it does best—if you are willing to put in the effort to change your thinking.

As you strive to change your thinking, tell yourself these three things:

- Change is Personal — I *need* to change.
- Change is Possible — I'm *able* to change.
- Change is Profitable — I'll be *rewarded* by change.

Remember, no matter how old you are or what your circumstances may be, you can change your thinking. And when you change your thinking, you change your beliefs.

Step 2: Changing Your Beliefs Changes Your Expectations

Billionaire entrepreneur Richard M. DeVos says, "The only thing that stands between a man and what he wants from life is often merely the will to try it and the faith to believe that it is possible."

A belief is not just an idea that you possess; it is an idea that possesses you. A belief holds great power, because it changes an individual's expectations. When Karen Ford changed her thinking and built

> A belief is not just an idea that you possess; it is an idea that possesses you.

her beliefs on a new foundation of growth, she had more than just hope and a dream to carry her forward. She expected to achieve her goal because she had done the hard work of changing to prepare for it. And she had prepared her people for it as well. They expected to succeed, and they did. The words of author Nelson Boswell are true: "The first and most important step toward success is the expectation that we can succeed."

Step 3: Changing Your Expectations Changes Your Attitude

A man walked into a fortune teller's tent at a carnival and paid his money to have his palm read.

"I see many things," she said.

"Like what?" the man asked.

"You will be poor and unhappy until you are forty-five," she stated.

"Oh," he said dejectedly. Then he had a thought. "What will happen when I'm forty-five?"

"You will get used to it."

Our expectations have a tremendous impact on our attitudes. Ben Franklin quipped, "Blessed is he who expects nothing, for he shall receive it." Negative expectations are a quick route to dead-end thinking. How many successful people do you know who are apathetic or negative? Positive expectations bring a positive attitude. They produce excitement, conviction, desire, confidence, commitment, and energy—all characteristics that help a person to achieve success. If you would like to possess these qualities in greater abundance, then raise your expectations.

> Negative expectations are a quick route to dead-end thinking.

Step 4: Changing Your Attitude Changes Your Behavior

Have you ever observed how your mood affects the way you act? When you feel particularly happy, are you more energized? Are you more likely to be kind to others? Do you take on tasks more readily and complete them with confidence and competence? How about when you're having a really bad day? Do you get less work done? Are you less patient with your family and colleagues? Does everything seem like a chore? Clergyman Earl Riney stated, "Our emotions are the driving powers of our lives."

What is an attitude? I believe . . .

It is the "advance man" of our true selves.
Its roots are inward but its fruit is outward.

It is our best friend or our worst enemy.
It is more honest and more consistent than our words.
It is an outward look based on past experiences.
It is a thing which draws people to us or repels them.
It is never content until it is expressed.
It is the librarian of our past.
It is the speaker of our present.
It is the prophet of our future.[11]

An attitude is little more than a mood or predominant emotion sustained over time. Psychologist William James said, "That which holds our attention determines our action." In other words, your behavior follows your attitude. The two cannot be separated. As author LeRoy Eims says, "How can you know what is in your heart? Look at your behavior."

Step 5: Changing Your Behavior Changes Your Performance

In my twenties, I decided to become a better golfer. I enjoyed the game, especially the mental challenge of it, but my performance left a lot to be desired. So I visited a golf professional to get some advice on how to improve.

My golf game suffered from a number of things, but the most serious problem was my grip. "You're using a baseball grip," the pro told me. "You're never going to improve until you change it." Then he showed me the proper way to hold the club.

"That feels terrible," I said. "Is this right?"

"That's it," he responded.

> Don't ever be too impressed with goal setting.
> Be impressed with goal getting.

"I don't know if I'll ever be able to do it this way," I complained.

"It's up to you," he answered. "You can do it the old way, but you'll never get any better." My performance depended on a change in behavior. I made the change.

Don't ever be too impressed with goal setting; be impressed with goal *getting*. Reaching new goals and moving to a higher level of performance always requires change, and change feels awkward. But, take comfort in the knowledge that if a change doesn't feel uncomfortable, then it's probably not really a change.

Step 6: Changing Your Performance Changes Your Life

When you change your performance—that is, what you do on a consistent basis—then you have the power to change your life. That was certainly true for Karen Ford. That's also been true for me. Although I write a lot of books, I'm primarily a speaker. Over the years, I've spoken for Peter Lowe at his Success seminars. I've addressed more than 50,000 people at a time in football stadiums. I've been on *Good Morning America*. I've spoken at the NCAA Final Four, the Indianapolis 500, and the NBA All Star Game. Each year I speak in person to more than 350,000 people. I don't tell you this to brag. I do it to let you know that when I say I'm a communicator, it really is true. My life bears it out.

Now, if you had heard me speak three and a half decades ago, you never would have expected me to have such a career. Let's just say I was less than inspiring. And if I had stayed the same, I never would have spoken to more than the few hundred people I had in my first church. But I desired to reach my potential, to go to the highest level of which I was capable. I was determined to improve.

To achieve a change in my performance, I first changed my thinking. I knew that I could not approach communication in the same way mentally and still perform differently. I began by studying speakers respected in my limited circle of experience and watching what they did. I tried to figure out what they were doing, then I copied them. I got better, but I still had a long way to go.

Next I took a more intellectual route to communication. I used research, statistics, and etymology. In the process I learned a little more, particularly when it came to preparation and writing. With those skills under my belt, I began to explore more broadly. I began studying people on a level of skill beyond anyone in my circle. I saw how they connected with an audience and I began trying to do the same. I realized that people learned better with some kind of hook. I saw how people responded to humor, and incorporated the kind of humor I could master. I kept adding to the mental side of communication, which ultimately improved my performance.

This may sound odd, but it took me eight years to learn how to be myself before an audience and to develop my own style. The whole process challenged me tremendously. And at times it felt terribly lonely. I felt as if I were the only person in the world who ever had to suffer through all these changes, even though intellectually I knew that I wasn't. Becoming a better communicator required a whole new way of thinking, and it felt uncomfortable. But I did it.

In the twenty-five years since then, I've continued to work at honing my skills and improving. I'm still a student of communication and I still try to learn from people better than I am. My basic style hasn't changed, but my thinking continues to evolve. I know that if I keep improving my thinking, it will impact my beliefs, which change my expectations, which affect my attitude, which changes my behavior, which improves my performance. And that will change my life.

THE NEXT LEVEL

Progress always requires change. Going to a new level always requires changing your mind. You may know that intuitively, but you need to make that idea foundational to the way you "do" life. Martin Grunder tells a story about Mark Victor Hansen, the motivational speaker who created the *Chicken Soup for the Soul* empire. Years ago, before his great success, Hansen approached Tony Robbins at an event where both of them were speaking. "Tony," he said, "I've been doing this for a long time and I'm doing okay. I'm making about a million dollars a year doing what I'm doing. I know for a fact that you made $156 million last year with your speaking and teaching and all of your products. How do you do it? How can I do it?"

Grunder says Robbins turned to Hansen and asked, "Who is in your mastermind group?" That's a group of like-minded people who meet to generate ideas and have accountability.

"Millionaires," replied Hansen. "We're all millionaires."

"That's what you're doing wrong," Robbins remarked. "You need to find yourself some billionaires and begin associating with them! *They'll get you thinking at their level.*"[12] To say that Hansen has gone to another level since that conversation is stating it mildly. His goal is to sell one billion *Chicken Soup* books, and he is well on his way to reaching that target.

If you want to *live* on a new level, you have to *think* on a new level. Recently I was talking to my old friend Bob Taylor, the founder of Taylor Guitars. Bob is a genius when it comes to manufacturing; he just happens to make guitars because he loves them. Bob invents most of the manufacturing equipment used to design and build the guitars his company sells. As much as anyone I know, he understands the value of good thinking. "In the end," Bob observed, "clear and inspired thinking is the only way to change things for the better. Someone asked me once, when I succeeded at a project that I had failed at before, 'What did you change?' I answered, 'I changed my mind.'"

Do you want to succeed where you have failed before? Do you want to go to a level you never even dreamed possible? Do you want to become the person you always hoped you could be? If you do, don't start by trying to change your actions. Start by changing your mind. Nothing else you do will have as great an impact.

THINKING QUESTION

Is my desire for success and to improve my life strong enough to prompt me to change my thinking?

Measuring the Impact of Changed Thinking

1. When Karen Ford faced obstacles in her path to the next level and failed, she almost quit. How have you handled similar situations? List several major disappointments you've faced in your career or personal life and how you responded.

_____

_____

2. When you have tried to improve your life in the past, where have you focused your energy? Using the list below, rank where you ordinarily place the most emphasis by marking it with a "1." Mark the next most important area with a "2," and proceed until you have ranked all six.

___ Thinking
___ Beliefs
___ Expectations
___ Attitude
___ Behavior
___ Performance

Based on your answers, how much will you have to change the way you naturally want to do things in order to change your thinking? Explain.

_____

_____

3. Success is OK so long as it's seen as growth, not an end in itself. Could your past successes be getting in the way of your future success? Think about an area where you have succeeded in the past but have currently plateaued. Figure out what is lacking in your current performance and trace back through performance, behavior, attitude, expectations, and beliefs until you reach the source: thinking. How must you change your thinking to break through to the next level?

_____

_____

Chapter 3

Master the Process of Intentional Thinking

"For the Flower to blossom, you need the right soil as well as the right seed. The same is true to cultivate good thinking."
—WILLIAM BERNBACH

What Were They Thinking?

"Half of this game is ninety percent mental."
—DANNY OZARK, Manager of the Philadelphia Phillies

The president of a company was showing a newly hired junior executive around the office. As they walked around, the two men passed a large corner office where a woman sat in a comfortable chair, looking out the window. The office had no desk, no computer, no file cabinets, nor any other equipment or tools normally contained in a working environment.

"Excuse me, sir," said the newly hired man. "But why isn't that office being used?"

"But it is," answered the president.

"Oh—well, I didn't see a desk or anything, so I thought maybe it was in transition. Who was sitting in the chair?"

"That's one of our vice presidents. It's her office," explained the president.

"What does she do for the company?"

"Think," answered the president with a smile.

"You pay her just to think? You mean, she doesn't have to *produce* anything? Wow, I'd love to have a job like that."

"The last idea she gave us *produced* $20 million for this company. Be able to do that on a consistent basis, and someday you just might have a job like hers."

Good thinkers are always in demand. A person who knows *how* may always have a job, but the person who knows *why* will always be his boss. Good thinkers solve problems, they never lack ideas that can build an organization, and they always have hope for a better future. Good thinkers rarely find themselves at the mercy of ruthless people who would take advantage of them or try to deceive them, people like Nazi dictator Adolf Hitler, who once boasted, "What luck for rulers that men do not think." Those who develop the process of good thinking can rule themselves—even while under an oppressive ruler or in other difficult circumstances.

> Good thinkers are always in demand. A person who knows *how* may always have a job, but the person who knows *why* will always be his boss.

Putting Yourself in the Right Place to Think

Becoming a good thinker isn't overly complicated. It's a discipline. And like most disciplines, it can be cultivated and refined. That's why I want to teach you the process that I've used to discover and develop good thoughts. It's certainly not the only one that works, but it has worked well for me.

1. Find a Place to Think Your Thoughts

I once heard that Charles Kettering, the great inventor and founder of Delco, who held more than 140 patents and received honorary doctorates from nearly 30 universities, talked about creating a place for thinking. He likened it to hanging a birdcage in one's mind. It seems a rather odd way of saying it, but the idea becomes clearer when you hear about a $100 bet he once made. Kettering told a friend that he could make the man buy a pet bird in the coming year. The friend figured that no one could *make* him do such a thing, so he took the bet.

Soon afterward, Kettering gave the man an expensive, handmade Swiss birdcage. The man took it home, and because it was so beautiful, he hung it in his dining room. But he found that every time he had guests over, someone would ask him, "When did your bird die?"

"I never had a bird," he'd tell them. Then he would have to explain the whole thing. After doing this repeatedly, he finally went out and bought a parakeet—and paid Kettering the $100 he owed him. Kettering later said, "If you hang birdcages in your mind, you eventually get something to put in them."

As Kettering's birdcage attracted a bird, so too will a designated place to think attract good thoughts. If you go to your thinking place expecting to generate good thoughts, then eventually you will come up with some.

For years, my goal has been to come up with one good thought every day. Now, that may not seem like much, but if you were able to do that five days a week for twelve months, you'd have over *two hundred fifty* good thoughts every year!

Where is the best place to think? Everybody's different. Some people think best in the shower. Others, like my friend Dick Biggs, like to go to a park. For me, the best places to think are:

- *In My Car:* I get lots of uninterrupted think time in my car. I don't give out the phone number of my car's cell phone, which is easy, because I don't even know it! While I'm driving, I'm usually either listening to tapes or giving concentrated think time to something specific.

- *On Planes:* Because of my speaking schedule, I spend quite a bit of time on planes. Occasionally, if one of my staff members needs to meet with me, I'll have him come along so we can talk. More often than not, I either read to generate ideas or spend the time jotting down thoughts and reflecting.

- *In My Spa:* One of my favorite places in the world is the spa in my back yard. Just about every day, I enjoy the relaxing warm water, reflect on my day, and spend time praying.

Ideas come to me in other places as well, such as when I'm in bed. (I keep a special lighted writing pad on my night stand for such times.) I believe I often get thoughts because I make it a habit to frequently

> When I found a place to think my thoughts, my thoughts found a place in me.

go to my thinking places. If you want to consistently generate ideas, you need to do the same thing. Find a place where you can think, and plan to capture your thoughts on paper so that you don't lose them. When I found a place to think my thoughts, my thoughts found a place in me.

2. Find a Place to Shape Your Thoughts

Rarely do ideas come fully formed and completely worked out. Most of the time, they need to be shaped until they have substance. As my friend Dan Reiland says, they have to "stand the test of clarity and questioning." During the shaping time, you want to hold an idea up to strong scrutiny. Many times a thought that seemed outstanding late at night looks pretty silly in the light of day.

Ask questions about your ideas. Fine tune them. One of the best ways to do that is to put your thoughts in writing. Professor, college president, and U.S. Senator S. I. Hayakawa wrote, "Learning to write is learning to think. You don't know anything clearly unless you can state it in writing."

> "Learning to write is learning to think. You don't know anything clearly unless you can state it in writing."
> —S. I. Hayakawa

As you shape your thoughts, you find out whether an idea has potential. You learn what you have. You also learn some things about yourself. The shaping time thrills me because it embodies:

- *Humor:* The thoughts that don't work often provide comic relief.

- *Humility:* The moments when I connect with God awe me.

- *Excitement:* I love to play out an idea mentally. (I call it "futuring" it.)

- *Creativity:* In these moments I am unhampered by reality.

- *Fulfillment:* God made me for this process; it uses my greatest gifts and gives me joy.

- *Honesty:* As I turn over an idea in my mind, I discover my true motives.

- *Passion:* When you shape a thought, you find out what you believe and what really counts.

- *Change:* Most of the changes I have made in my life resulted from thorough thinking on a subject.

The shaping phase of thinking has left a great mark on me. During this phase, I have experienced my highest and lowest moments. During such times over the years, I received my calling into the ministry, God broke and humbled me, my convictions were formed, and my priorities became clear and established. Other times, I've recognized my failures as a leader or deficiencies as a husband. And I've also celebrated a few successes. Who I am today is a result of my thought-shaping times. I still get a rush whenever I spend quality time thinking and reflecting.

I've shaped my thoughts in many places. While working on my bachelor's degree, I visited an old house made of cinder blocks at Circleville Bible College. Right after I got married and began working in my first job, I spent a lot of time sitting on a rock behind my house in Hillham, Indiana. When I lived in Lancaster, Ohio, I'd go to a park. In San Diego, I visited a place in my church I called the "upper room." And today, I shape ideas in my home office or when I spend time in the mountains of the Carolinas.

You can shape your thoughts almost anywhere. Just find a place that works for you, where you will be able to write things down, focus your attention without interruptions, and ask questions about your ideas. As Dave Sutherland, president of INJOY Stewardship Services says, "Sometimes the questions you ask are more important than the answers you receive." By asking questions, you gain perspective on your ideas. As I have tried to shape my thoughts, I have often realized that my thoughts have shaped me.

3. Find a Place to Stretch Your Thoughts

If you come upon great thoughts and spend time mentally shaping them, don't think you're done and can stop there. If you do, you will miss some of the most valuable aspects of the thinking process. You miss bringing others in and expanding ideas to their greatest potential.

Earlier in my life, I have to admit, I was often guilty of this error. I wanted to take an idea from seed thought to solution before sharing it with anyone, even the people it would most impact. I did this both at work and at home. But over the years, I have learned that you can go much farther with a team than you can go alone.

I wholeheartedly embrace what I wrote in *The 17 Indisputable Laws of Teamwork*: "One is too small a number to achieve greatness." If you really want to take an idea to the highest level, ask others to help you.

I've found a kind of formula that can help you stretch your thoughts. It says,

The Right **Thought** plus the Right **People**
in the Right **Environment** at the Right **Time**
for the Right **Reason** = the **Right Result**

This combination is hard to beat. Here's why:

- *The Right Thought:* Everything must generally begin with the seed of an idea. As George Gardner once observed, "Thought is, perhaps, the forerunner and even the mother of ideas, and ideas are the most powerful and the most useful things in the world."

- *The Right People:* When you expose an idea to the right people, incredible things can happen. The original thought often grows, along with its vision, power, and impact. Who are the right people to stretch a vision? They are ones who love you and embrace your vision, who know you and strengthen your vision, and who complement you and enlarge your vision. They are the few who stretch a thought before you land it with many. Some of the people in my thinking life, and the areas where they stretch my thinking, include:

Bill Hybels — Leadership
Larry Maxwell — Business
Dan Cathy — Servanthood
Dave Sutherland — Strategy
John Hull — Relationships
Fred Smith — Insight
Kevin Small — Opportunity
Margaret Maxwell — Perspective
Tom Phillippe — Wisdom
Jim Dornan — Change
Pat Williams — Creativity
Bill Bright — Vision
Charlie Wetzel — Writing

The people in your life impact your thinking, for better or for worse, so why not work strategically to find people who will stretch you to your potential? Make it a goal to find people who will add value to you in areas that are important to you. (And make yourself available to do the same for others.) This will take your thinking to a whole new level.

- *The Right Environment:* Your environment will either stretch or shrink your ideas. In the right environment thinking is valued, ideas flow freely, fresh eyes are welcome, change is expected, questions are encouraged, egos are checked, ideas stimulate better ideas, and thinking generates teamwork. If you're stuck in a wrong environment, then find one that encourages you. If you are a leader, then realize that you are creating the environment you're in. The responsibility for making it better rests on you!

- *The Right Time:* Ideas are fragile things when they first see the light of day. If you try to implement them too early or introduce them while there are more naysayers than supporters, they won't survive. Emperor Hadrian of ancient Rome believed, "To be right too soon is to be wrong." While still in the stretching stage of an idea, present it without time frames or rigidly defined goals. Thoughts must be allowed to breathe before you harness them.

- *The Right Reason:* J. P. Morgan said, "A man always has two reasons for doing any thing: a good reason and the real reason." Motives matter. People usually feel more inclined to help stretch ideas that add value to others.

Like every person, every thought has the potential to become something great. When you find a place to stretch your thoughts, you find that potential. Sometimes a thought is merely a springboard to a greater idea, but without that springboard, the great idea will never be found. Sometimes a thought becomes great when it partners with another idea. And sometimes a thought excels just as it is and only needs to be fleshed out. Finding a place to stretch your thoughts gives you a chance to take that idea as far as it can go. As I have tried to stretch my thinking, I have discovered that my thinking has stretched me.

4. Find a Place to Land Your Thoughts

Author C. D. Jackson observes that "great ideas need landing gear as well as wings." Any idea that remains only an idea doesn't make a great impact. The real power of an idea comes when it goes from abstraction to application. Think about Einstein's theory of relativity. When he published his theories in 1905 and 1916, they were merely profound ideas. Their real power came with the development of the nuclear reactor in 1942 and the nuclear bomb in 1945. When scientists developed and implemented Einstein's ideas, the whole world changed.

Likewise, if you want your thoughts to make an impact, you need to land them with others so that they can someday be implemented. As you plan for the application phase of the thinking process, land your ideas first with . . .

- *Yourself:* Landing an idea with yourself will give you integrity. People will buy into an idea only after they buy into the leader who communicates it. That won't happen if the leader doesn't believe in it. Before teaching any lesson, I ask myself three questions: "Do I believe it? Do I live it? Do I believe others should live it?" If I can't answer yes to all three questions, then I haven't landed it.

- *Key Players:* Let's face it, no idea will fly if the influencers don't embrace it. After all, they are the people who carry thoughts from idea to implementation. Landing an idea with the influencers in your organization will increase your influence.

- *Those Most Affected:* Landing thoughts with the people on the firing line will give you great insight. Those closest to changes that occur as a result of a new idea can give you a "reality read." And that's important, because sometimes even when you've diligently completed the process of creating a thought, shaping it, and stretching it with other good thinkers, you can still miss the mark.

J. Jacobson remarked, "A good idea is like a wheelbarrow; it will go nowhere unless you push it." While that's true, there's more to landing an idea than simply pushing it. Your timing is important. As you prepare to present new ideas to people, keep in mind that they are most willing to embrace change when they:

- Hurt enough that they are willing to change.
- Learn enough that they want to change.
- Receive enough that they are able to change.

Present your ideas at one of those ideal moments, and you will more likely be able to take your thoughts to the final phase of the process. As I have tried to land my thoughts, I have understood that my thoughts have given me a secure foundation.

5. Find a Place to Fly Your Thoughts

French philosopher Henri-Louis Bergson, who won the Nobel Prize in literature in 1927, asserted that a person should "think like a man of action—act like a man of thought." What good is thinking if it has no application in real life? Thinking divorced from actions cannot be productive. Learning how to master the process of thinking well leads you to productive thinking. If you can develop the discipline of good thinking and turn it into a lifetime habit, then you will be productive all of your life. Once you've created, shaped, stretched, and landed your thoughts, then flying them can be fun and easy.

I've observed that high achievers have a natural tendency to jump into any project and start working; they are usually people of action who possess high energy. But to get the kind of results you want—to fly your thoughts well—you should give good thinking time to any endeavor.

Give your plans the right amount of thinking time, and you'll find that the implementation time decreases and the results get better. Your thinking time is like the runway of an airport. Just as larger planes need a longer runway to fly, big ideas need a long runway of thinking to get launched. As I have tried to fly my thoughts, I have found that my thoughts have taken me to new heights.

How to Become a Good Thinker

Do you want to master the process of good thinking? Then I recommend the following:

1. Expose Yourself to Good Input

Good thinkers always prime the pump of ideas. They always look for things to get the thinking process started. However, what you put in always impacts what comes out, as this poem called "Keeper of the Keys" illustrates:

You are the Keeper of The Keys.
You are the Guard at The Gate.
Waiting in line to get through that door
Is LOVE. And also HATE.
In line to enter is GENTLE PEACE.
And also VIOLENT WAR.
You must choose who may, and who
May not come through the door.
INTOLERANCE tries to sneak on through
On wings of FEAR, or PRIDE.
It hides behind DREAMS of BELONGING,
And tries to sneak inside.

Oh! Be alert! You're the Guard who decides
Who GOES and who may STAY.
You are The Keeper of The Keys to Your Mind.
Who will you let in today?[13]

Read books, review trade magazines, listen to tapes, and spend time with good thinkers. And when something intrigues you—whether it's someone else's idea or the seed of an idea that you've come up with yourself—keep it in front of you. Put it in writing and keep it somewhere in your favorite thinking place to stimulate your thinking.

I once kept a picture from a magazine on my desk for a year to keep me focused on a goal and to stimulate my thinking about how I might accomplish it. But my favorite place to keep ideas that need reflection is a half-sheet sized portfolio that I keep with me. It's my thinking companion. After I flesh out an idea and write a first draft outlining it, I'll place it in the portfolio on the left-hand side. (The right-hand side has blank pages where I capture new ideas.) Periodically, I'll look at the draft, give it more thought time, and revise it. Right now, my thinking companion contains five projects that I have been revisiting. One of them has been there for nine months! They will all stay there until they are ready to be launched. This process allows my thinking to simmer in the crock pot of my mind until the ideas are "done."

2. Expose Yourself to Good Thinkers

Spend time with the right people. As I worked on this chapter and bounced my ideas off of some key people (so that my thoughts would be stretched), I realized something about myself. All of the people in my life whom I consider to be close friends or colleagues are thinkers. Now, I love all people.

I try to be kind to everyone I meet, and I desire to add value to as many people as I can through conferences, books, lessons on tape, etc. But the people I seek out and choose to spend time with all challenge me with their thinking and their actions. They are constantly trying to grow and learn. That's true of my wife, Margaret, my close friends, and the executives who run my companies. Every one of them is a good thinker!

> If you want to be a sharp thinker, be around sharp people.

The writer of Proverbs observed that sharp people sharpen one another, just as iron sharpens iron. If you want to be a sharp thinker, be around sharp people.

3. Choose to Think Good Thoughts

To become a good thinker, you must become intentional about the thinking process. Regularly put yourself in the right place to think, shape, stretch, and land your thoughts. Make it a priority. Remember, thinking is a discipline.

Recently I had breakfast with Dan Cathy, the president of Chick-fil-A, a fast food chain headquartered in the Atlanta area. I told him that I was working on this book and I asked him if he made thinking time a high priority. Not only did he say yes, but he told me about what he calls his "thinking schedule." It helps him to fight the hectic pace of life that discourages intentional thinking. Dan says he sets aside time just to think for half a day every two weeks, for one whole day every month, and for two or three full days every year. Dan explains, "This helps me 'keep the main thing, the main thing,' since I am so easily distracted."

You may want to do something similar, or you can develop a schedule and method of your own. No matter what you choose to do, go to your thinking place, take paper and pen, and make sure you capture your ideas in writing.

4. Act on Your Good Thoughts

Ideas have a short shelf life. You must act on them before the expiration date. World War I flying ace Eddie Rickenbacker said it all when he remarked, "I can give you a six-word formula for success: Think things through—then follow through."

> Ideas have a short shelf life. You must act on them before the expiration date.

5. Allow Your Emotions to Create Another Good Thought

I counseled many people as a pastor. In that process, I discovered that for some people, the greatest challenge to becoming a good thinker is their emotional turmoil or baggage. Past hurts or current worries prevent them from spending productive time thinking.

To start the thinking process, you cannot rely on your feelings. In *Failing Forward*, I wrote that you can act your way into feeling long before you can feel your way into action. If you wait until you *feel* like doing something, you will likely never accomplish it. The same is true for thinking. You cannot wait until you feel like thinking to do it. However, I've found that once you engage in the process of good thinking, you can use your emotions to feed the process and create mental momentum.

Try it for yourself. After you go through the disciplined process of thinking and enjoy some success, allow yourself to savor the moment and try riding the mental energy of that success. If you're like me, it's likely to spur additional thoughts and productive ideas.

6. Repeat the Process

A few weeks ago, I had lunch with an old friend named David Dean. He and I don't see each other very often, but we grew

51

up together as kids. We attended the same college and shared many memorable experiences. Today he is a very successful pastor in Ohio. As we sat down together over lunch, we talked over old times and caught up on mutual friends. Then he recounted a conversation we had in 1979 over dinner at a Holiday Inn in Wapokenetta, Ohio. I didn't recall it, but he did.

"I remember it like it was yesterday," Dave remarked. "You said that you planned to make it a practice to read and think every day." In 1979, he and I would have been in our early thirties. That was about the time that I realized the key to achieving success was to keep growing and improving. It's something that has been a part of my life ever since. Sometimes keeping myself on a growth plan has been fun. Other times it's been drudgery. But I've persevered, and I believe it is one of the reasons I've been able to keep writing books and speaking for more than twenty years.

"John," my friend said, "there's something else you said back then. You told me your goal was to fill your mind with so much good stuff, that by the time you're fifty-five, it just flows out of you when you speak."

"What?" I asked, a little confused. "What did I say?"

Dave repeated it for me. I felt stunned. "Dave," I said, "you won't believe this. I turned fifty-five yesterday."

Tears filled my eyes. David's voice cracked as he said, "John, it's really worked. With all the speaking and the books you've done, it's actually happened."

People make a lot of little decisions in life. Most of the time, you make them, forget them, and move on. You hope that they will make an impact, but you often don't examine how they shape your life. What a wonderful gift to be reminded that a decision to grow and think more than twenty years ago is making a difference in my life today!

One good thought does not make a good life. The people who

have one good thought and try to ride it for an entire career often end up unhappy or destitute. They are the one-hit won-ders, the one-book authors, the one-message speakers, the one-time inventors who spend their life struggling to protect or promote their single idea. Success comes to

> One good thought does not make a life. Success comes to those who have an entire mountain of gold that they continuously mine.

those who have an entire mountain of gold that they continu-ally mine, not those who find one nugget and try to live on it for fifty years. To become someone who can mine a lot of gold, you need to keep repeating the process of good thinking.

THE IDEAS KEEP ON COMING

Someone who keeps mining nuggets of idea gold is my friend Dick Biggs. Dick is a magazine publisher, speaker, and author who has helped me do some of the thinking for this book.

I recently asked him to tell me about one of the best thoughts he ever had. Without hesitation, he named the idea for "Burn Brightly Without Burning Out." That idea became a little booklet for Successories. Dick has been training people and speaking to businesses for twenty years. He's done a lot of things, and he's highly successful. But after writing that book, he has received an overwhelming number of requests to talk about the subject. Now he's writing a trade book based on the idea.

The whole thing started as a little idea, the kind of thing most people forget, dismiss, or allow to slip away. Dick has grown it into something that not only has impacted his own life, but those of the many people he speaks to at conferences and seminars. And he just keeps on mining. Who knows what his next great idea will be!

It doesn't matter whether you were born rich or poor. It doesn't matter if you have a third grade education or possess a Ph.D. It doesn't matter if you suffer from multiple disabilities or you're the picture of health. No matter what your circumstances, you can learn to be a good thinker. All you must do is be willing to engage in the process every day.

THINKING QUESTION

Am I willing to pay the price to cultivate the habit of giving birth to, nurturing, and developing great thoughts every day?

Putting Good Thinking into Action

1. If you don't already have a good thinking place, you need to find one. Where will you choose to create your thoughts?

_____

_____

_____

2. Who are the good thinkers in your life? List them here:

_____

_____

_____

3. What are you currently working on that could benefit from some think time? You may want to address the issue you iden-

tified at the end of Chapter 1. As clearly as you can, write down the problem here.

_____

_____

_____

4. Spend some time thinking about that issue. Then get together the good thinkers in your life to help you stretch and then land your thoughts.

_____

_____

_____

5. To what good input are you regularly exposing yourself? Do you have a plan for growth? To what magazines, journals, or tape services do you subscribe, just to challenge yourself as a thinker? List them here.

_____

_____

_____

If you don't already get such input, then begin immediately. List three to five resources that you can begin using to improve yourself.

_____

_____

_____

_____

_____

PART II

ELEVEN THINKING SKILLS EVERY

SUCCESSFUL PERSON NEEDS

Skill 1

Acquire the Wisdom of Big-Picture Thinking

> *"Where success is concerned, people are not measured in inches, or pounds, or college degrees, or family background; they are measured by the size of their thinking."*
> —DAVID SCHWARTZ

What Were They Thinking?

> *"Outside of the killings, Washington has one of the lowest crime rates in the country."*
> —MARION BARRY,
> former Washington, D.C., mayor

If someone told you that on the longest day of the year you would be able to look deep into an old-fashioned well and see the sun reflected in the water, what would you think? Would you consider that an interesting but useless piece of trivia? Would you think the person who noticed the reflection needed to get a life? Or would it stir ideas that would challenge your paradigm about the world?

The Big Picture Is a Ball

An Egyptian librarian heard that bit of information—that the sun could be seen shining at the bottom of a well in the town of Syene—and he considered it more than mere trivia. That detail about the well started this big-picture thinker thinking. He surmised that if it made a reflection in a well, the sun must be directly overhead. And if it were directly overhead, then it would cast no shadows from upright columns or posts. Yet on the longest day of the year in the city of Alexandria, where he lived, he observed that straight columns did cast shadows.

As a good scientist and thinker, he decided to travel 800 kilometers to Syene to verify that what he had heard was true. On the longest day of the year, he looked into the well and saw the sun reflected. And sure enough, at midday, posts cast no shadows. So he began thinking. After a while, he started to see a bigger picture of what these seemingly insignificant facts meant. Surprisingly, it went against what nearly everyone believed at the time. You see, the librarian's name was Eratosthenes, and he lived more than 2,200 years ago.

As the director of the greatest library in the world (the library of Alexandria in Egypt was said to possess hundreds of thousands of scrolls), he was at the intellectual capital of the planet. In the third century B.C., nearly every scholar in Alexandria and around the world believed the earth to be flat. But Eratosthenes reasoned that if the sun's light came down straight and the earth was flat, then there would be no shadows in either location. If there were shadows in one location but not the other, then there could be only one logical explanation. The surface of the earth must be curved. In other words, the world must be a sphere.

BROAD HORIZONS

That's a pretty impressive mental leap, although it seems perfectly logical today. After all, we've seen pictures of our planet from space. But Eratosthenes made that big-picture connection by using everyday facts and putting them together. Even more impressive, he took it one step further. He actually calculated the size of the earth! Using basic trigonometry, he measured the angle of the shadows: approximately 7.12 degrees, about 1/50th of a circle. Then he reasoned that if the distance between Syene (modern-day Aswan) and Alexandria was 800 kilometers (using our standards of measurement), then the earth must be around 40,000 kilometers in circumference (50 x 800 kilometers). He wasn't far off; the actual circumference of the earth through the poles is 40,008 kilometers. Not bad for a guy who had nothing but his brain and a big-picture mind-set to figure the whole thing out!

In the actions of Eratosthenes, you can see the truth of a statement made centuries later by German statesman Konrad Adenauer: "We all live under the same sky, but we don't all have the same horizon." How many thousands of people had seen what Eratosthenes saw and never made the same connection? How many hundreds of his fellow *mathematicians* saw the same shadows he did and failed to see the big picture? Eratosthenes wasn't even the most talented mathematician of his day. His peers called him *beta* and *pentathlos,* which is kind of like calling him "Mr. Second Place."[14] But that didn't matter. Though he wasn't the top man in any discipline, he could see—and think—big picture. And that's the reason his name is remembered today. Using that ability, he not only calculated the circumference of the earth, but he also accurately sketched the route of the Nile River, worked out a calendar that included leap years, and estimated the earth's distance from the sun and moon. Eratosthenes certainly didn't get caught up in the trees and miss the forest. In fact, his perspective was so good that he saw not only the forest, but also the river that flowed into it, the planet that contained them, and parts of the solar system to which the planet belonged!

THE MINDSET OF BIG-PICTURE THINKERS

You don't have to be a scientist or mathematician to embrace big-picture thinking or to benefit from it. It can help any person in any profession. When somebody like Jack Welch tells a GE employee that the ongoing relationship with the customer is more important than the sale of an individual product, he's reminding them of the big picture. When my friend Andy Stanley, senior pastor of North Point Community Church, asks his volunteers to give their best in service every Sunday for the sake of the first-time visitor hoping to find a culturally relevant church, he is painting the big picture for them. When two parents are fed up with potty training, poor grades, or fender-benders, and one reminds the other that the current difficult time is only a temporary season, then they benefit from thinking big picture.

Real estate developer Donald Trump quipped, "You have to think anyway, so why not think big?" Big-picture thinking brings wholeness and maturity to a person's thinking. It brings perspective. It's like making the frame of a picture bigger, in the process expanding not only what you can see, but what you are able to do.

> "You have to think anyway, so why not think big?"
> —Donald Trump

Spend time with big-picture thinkers, and you will find that they:

Learn Continually

Big-picture thinkers are never satisfied with what they already know. They are always visiting new places, reading new books, meeting new people, learning new skills. And because of that practice, they often are able to connect the unconnected, just as Eratosthenes did. They are life-long learners.

To help me maintain a learner's attitude, I spend a few moments every morning thinking about my learning opportunities for the day. As I review my calendar and to-do list—knowing whom I will meet that day, what I will read, which meetings I will attend—I note where I am most likely to learn something. Then I mentally cue myself to look attentively for something that will improve me in that situation. If you desire to keep learning, I want to encourage you to examine your day and look for opportunities to learn.

Listen Intentionally

An excellent way to broaden your experience is to listen to someone who has expertise in an area where you don't. I search for such opportunities. This year I spoke to about 900 coaches and scouts at the Senior Bowl, where graduating football players participate in their last college game. I had the opportunity, along with my son-in-law, Steve Miller, to have dinner with NFL head coaches Dave Wannstedt and Butch Davis. It's not often that you get such an opportunity, so I asked them questions about teamwork and spent a lot of time listening to them.

At the end of the evening, as Steve and I were walking to our car, he said to me, "John, I bet you asked those coaches a hundred questions tonight."

"If I'm going to learn and grow," I replied, "I must know what questions to ask and know how to apply the answers to my life. Listening has taught me a lot more than talking."

When you meet with people, it's good to have an agenda so that you can learn. It's a great way to partner with people who can do things you can't. Big-picture thinkers recognize that they don't know lots of things. They frequently ask penetrating questions to enlarge their understanding and thinking. If you want to become a better big-picture thinker, then become a good listener.

Look Expansively

Writer Henry David Thoreau wrote, "Many an object is not seen, though it falls within the range of our visual ray, because it does not come within the range of our intellectual ray." Human beings habitually see their own world first. For example, when people arrive at a leadership conference put on by my company, INJOY, they want to know where they're going to park, whether they will be able to get a good (and comfortable) seat, whether the speaker will be "on," and if the breaks will be spaced right. When I arrive to speak at the same conference, I want to know that the lighting is good, the sound equipment is operating effectively, whether the speaker's platform will be close enough to the people, etc. Who you are determines what you see—and how you think.

Big-picture thinkers realize there is a world out there besides their own, and they make an effort to get outside of themselves and see other people's worlds through their eyes. It's hard to see the picture while inside the frame. To see how others see, you must first find out how they think. Becoming a good listener certainly helps with that. So does getting over your personal agenda and trying to take the other person's perspective.

Live Completely

French essayist Michel Eyquem de Montaigne wrote, "The value of life lies not in the length of days, but in the use we make of them; a man may live long yet live very little." The truth is that you can spend your life any way you want, but you can spend it only once. Becoming a big-picture thinker can help you to live with wholeness, to live a very fulfilling life. People who see the big picture expand their experience because they expand their world. As a result, they accomplish more than narrow minded people. And they experience fewer unwanted surprises, too, because they are more likely to see the many components involved in any given situation: issues, people, relationships, timing, and values. They are also, therefore, usually more tolerant of other people and their thinking.

> The truth is that you can spend your life any way you want, but you can spend it only once.

WHY YOU SHOULD RECEIVE THE WISDOM OF BIG-PICTURE THINKING

Intuitively, you probably recognize big-picture thinking as beneficial. Few people *want* to be closed-minded. No one sets out to be that way. But just in case you're not completely convinced, consider several specific reasons why you should make the effort to become a better big-picture thinker:

1. Big-Picture Thinking Allows You to Lead

A few years ago in *Leadership* journal, Lynn Anderson described an incident from American history to illustrate limited thinking. More than three centuries ago, the Pilgrims landed on the shores of the American continent with great courage and vision. In their first year, a small group of settlers established a town. The next year, they elected a town council. In their third year, that council proposed building a road five miles into the wilderness for westward expansion. But the following year, the people criticized the proposal as a waste of public funds. Evidently they couldn't see the big picture. As Anderson pointed out, the Pilgrims had once been able to see across the oceans; they now could not look five miles into the wilderness.

You can find many big-picture thinkers who aren't leaders, but you will find few leaders who are not big-picture thinkers. Leaders must be able to do many important things for their people:

- *See the vision before their people do.* That's one of the reasons they are able to lead. Leaders not only see the big picture before others do, they also see more of it. This allows them to . . .

- *Size up situations, taking into account many variables.* Leaders who see the big picture discern possibilities as well as problems. As Max De Pree says, the first responsibility of a leader is to define reality. Doing that allows the leader to form a foundation to build the vision. Once leaders have done that, they can . . .

- *Sketch a picture of where the team is going.* Too often when people present the big picture, it is drawn up as a bright image without any challenges or obstacles. That false portrait leads only to discouragement when followers actually take the journey. The goal of leaders shouldn't be merely to make their people feel good, but to help them be good and accomplish the dream. The vision, shown accurately, will allow leaders to . . .

- *Show how the future connects with the past to make the journey more meaningful.* Most people want to touch their past before they will reach out to their future. When they can do that, moving forward seems natural and right. When leaders recognize this need for connection and bridge it, then they can . . .

- *Seize the moment when the timing is right.* In leadership, when to move is as important as what you do. As Winston Churchill said, "There comes a special moment in everyone's life, a moment for which that person was born. . . . When he seizes it . . . it is his finest hour."

Whether building roads, planning a trip, or moving in leadership, big-picture thinking allows you to enjoy more success. People who are constantly looking at the whole picture have the best chance of succeeding in any endeavor.

2. Big-Picture Thinking Keeps You on Target

Thomas Fuller, chaplain to Charles II of England, observed, "He that is everywhere is nowhere." To get things done, you need focus. However, to get the right things done, you also need to consider the big picture. Only by putting your daily activities in the context of the big picture will you be able to stay on target. As Alvin Toffler says, "You've got to think about 'big things' while you're doing small things, so that all the small things go in the right direction."

> "You've got to think about 'big things' while you're doing small things, so that all the small things go in the right direction."
> —Alvin Toffler

3. Big-Picture Thinking Allows You to See What Others See

One of the most important skills you can develop in human relations is the ability to see things from the other person's point of view. It's one of the keys to working with clients, satisfying customers, maintaining a marriage, rearing children, helping those who are less fortunate, etc. All human interactions are enhanced by the ability to put yourself in another person's shoes.

How do you do that? How do you get outside of yourself and look at things from another perspective? You look beyond yourself, your own interests, and your own world. You look at the big picture. When you work to consider an issue from every possible angle, examine it in the light of another's history, discover the interests and concerns of others, and try to set aside your own agenda, you begin to see what others see. And that is a powerful thing.

4. Big-Picture Thinking Promotes Teamwork

If you participate in any kind of team activity, then you know how important it is that team members see the whole picture, not just their own part. Anytime a person doesn't know how his work fits with that of his teammates, then the whole team is in trouble. The better the grasp team members have of the big picture, the greater their potential to work together as a team.

Consider how people work together during halftime at a college football bowl game. If you've attended a game, then you—along with everyone else in the stadium—were probably instructed to hold up a solid-colored card during the halftime show. Alone, the card looks like nothing. Even a hundred cards together don't show much. But for anyone who can see the whole stadium, it's obvious that all the cards together spell out a message. When team members see the big picture, they all get the message.

5. Big-Picture Thinking Keeps You from Being Caught Up in the Mundane

Let's face it: some aspects of everyday life are absolutely necessary but thoroughly uninteresting. Big-picture thinkers don't let the grind get to them, because they don't lose sight of the all-important overview. They know that the person who forgets the ultimate is a slave to the immediate.

I begin each day with a big-picture mindset. To accomplish this, I look at my written agenda for the day. It allows me to see the whole day at a glance. Out of my schedule, I pick out the "main event," the one thing most important for me to do well, the thing that will make or break my day.

In preparation for the day, I focus on that main event and ask myself, *In order to make the main event a good event, what must I know, what must I do, what must I see, and what must I eliminate?* Once I answer these questions, I am able to approach my day with a big-picture perspective. Some things will be fun; some things won't. But with preparation, the most important thing will be done well.

6. Big-Picture Thinking Helps You to Chart Uncharted Territory

Have you ever heard the expression, "We'll cross that bridge when we come to it"? That phrase undoubtedly was coined by someone who had trouble seeing the big picture. The world was built by people who "crossed bridges" in their minds long before anyone else did. The only way to break new ground or move into uncharted territory is to look beyond the immediate and see the big picture.

Think about Christopher Columbus. When he and his crew sailed west in the *Niña*, the *Pinta*, and the *Santa Maria*, they journeyed under the flag of Queen Isabella of Spain, which bore the motto *Ne Plus Ultra*, meaning "nothing farther." When Columbus returned to the monarch with the report of his findings, the queen ordered the "Ne" removed so that the motto read *Plus Ultra*. It indicated that Columbus had charted uncharted territory, and now new horizons and new opportunities lay before those who desired to seize them.

HOW TO ACQUIRE THE WISDOM OF BIG-PICTURE THINKING

If you desire to seize new opportunities and open new horizons, then you need to add big-picture thinking to your abilities. To become a good thinker better able to see the big picture, keep in mind the following suggestions:

1. Don't Strive for Certainty

Big-picture thinkers are comfortable with ambiguity. They don't try to force every observation or piece of data into pre-formulated mental cubby holes. They think broadly and can juggle many seemingly contradictory thoughts in their minds.

Management consultant Patrick M. Lencioni touched on this idea in *The Five Temptations of a CEO*. He warned that CEOs should not try to pursue harmony. Instead, they should embrace healthy, productive conflict. Nor should they aim for certainty. Instead they should try to find clarity. If you want to cultivate the ability to think big picture, then you must get used to embracing and dealing with complex and diverse ideas. Get in the habit of bringing together diverse concepts, accepting seemingly opposite points of view at the same time, and embracing what authors James C. Collins and Jerry I. Porras call the "Genius of the AND." In business, for example, pursue purpose AND profit, embrace a fixed core ideology AND vigorous change and innovation, be highly visionary AND execute the details well.[15]

2. Learn from Every Experience

Big-picture thinkers broaden their outlook by striving to learn from every experience. They don't rest on their successes, they learn from them. More importantly, they learn from their failures. They can do that because they remain teachable.

In *Failing Forward*, a teachable spirit is described in this way:

> Teachability is an attitude, a mind-set that says, "No matter how much I know (or think I know), I can learn from this situation." That kind of thinking can help you turn adversity into advantage. It can make you a winner even during the most difficult circumstances.[16]

Varied experiences—both positive and negative—help you see the big picture. The greater the variety of experience and success, the more potential to learn you have. If you desire to be a big-picture thinker, then get out there and try a lot of things, take a lot of chances, and take time to learn after every victory or defeat.

3. Gain Insight from a Variety of People

Big-picture thinkers learn from their experiences. But they also learn from experiences they don't have. That is, they learn by receiving insight from others—from customers, employees, colleagues, and leaders. My friend Kevin Myers, who is in his early forties, meets with a group of younger men to mentor them and answer their questions and share his experiences. Every month or so, Kevin

> Big-picture thinkers learn from their experiences. But they also learn from experiences they don't have.

also meets me for lunch, armed with questions he wants to ask me. Does he do it because I'm more intelligent or talented than he is? No. I just have fifteen years more experience than he does, and he benefits from the lessons I've learned. And you already know that I also seek the counsel of people with varied experience (see Chapter 3).

If you desire to broaden your thinking and see more of the big picture, then seek out counselors to help you. But be wise in *whom* you ask for advice. One of my favorite "Peanuts" cartoon strips shows how much that matters. In the cartoon, Charlie Brown is holding up his hands and telling Lucy, "These are the hands which may someday accomplish great things. These are hands which may someday do marvelous works! They may build mighty bridges, or heal the sick, or hit home runs, or write soul-stirring novels! These are the hands which may someday change the course of destiny!" Lucy looks at his hands and simply says, "They've got jelly on them."

Gaining insight from a variety of people doesn't mean stopping anyone and everyone in hallways and grocery store lines and asking what they think about a given subject. Be selective. Talk to people who know and care about you, who know their field, and who bring experience deeper and broader than your own. (Knowing who you should select to give you counsel will be discussed in greater detail in the section on shared thinking.)

4. Give Yourself Permission to Expand Your World

If you want to be a big-picture thinker, you will have to go against the flow of the world. Society wants to keep people in boxes. Most people are married mentally to the *status quo.* They want what was, not what can be. They seek safety and simple answers. To think big-picture, you need to give yourself permission to go a different way, to break new ground, to find new worlds to conquer. And when your world does get bigger, you need to celebrate. Never forget there is more out there in the world than what you've experienced.

I grew up in a household where anything was possible, and we celebrated the big picture. So it flabbergasted me when I had my first major experience with minds unalterably closed. In happened one Sunday in August of 1969. Just a few weeks after getting married and graduating from college, I took my first job as a pastor in a small town in rural Indiana. Calling it a town is being generous. The place consisted of fourteen houses, a gas station, and a country store.

I'm a fan of progress, and I am a high believer in human potential. So I felt very excited on that Sunday when NASA was about to put a man on the moon for the first time in history. But an interesting thing happened that day. As I spoke to the people in my church about this major accomplishment, I could tell that I wasn't connecting with them. The more they just sat there, the more energetic and animated I got. But no matter how hard I tried, they just would not respond.

After the service, as I shook hands and chatted, I realized something shocking: they did not believe that a man was about to walk on the moon! One man told me, "If God had wanted a man on the moon, He would have put him there." It floored me. It was the first time I had encountered such small thinking.

Playwright Victor Hugo observed, "A small man is made up of small thoughts." I realized then that many of the town's residents had a very small view of the world. They had not altered their narrow thinking in years and they did not want to expand it.

How important it is to keep learning, keep growing, and keep looking at the big picture! If you desire to be a good thinker, that's what you need to do.

THINKING QUESTION

*Am I thinking beyond myself and my world
so that I process ideas with a holistic perspective?*

Putting Big-Picture Thinking into Action

1. On a scale of 1 to 10, with one being narrow and 10 being expansive, how do you rate as a big-picture thinker? Do you see the whole picture, or are you more likely to focus on just one aspect?

_____

_____

_____

If you scored a number lower than 8, give yourself permission to expand your world, and then tenaciously work at becoming a better big-picture thinker.

2. Pick a past problem or current project that you would like to improve through big-picture thinking. Then use the following exercises to expand your thinking:

1. *Opposites:* What is the obvious solution for success? Write it here:

_____

_____

Now, what is an alternate solution, something that would resolve the issue but seems to contradict the first idea? Write it here:

_____

_____

How can you make those seemingly contradictory ideas work together?

_____

_____

2. *Insight from Others:* Take that same issue, problem, or project to three to five people who can give you insight on it. Be sure to pick good people using the criteria in the chapter: they must know and care about you, know their field, and bring experience deeper and broader than yours. Before you meet with each of them, spend adequate time formulating the questions you want to ask. That process will help you clarify the issues, and it will show your friends how much you respect their time.

3. Make learning from your experiences a regular part of your daily routine. Set aside a few minutes at the end of each day (or first thing the next morning) to review what you learn each day. Capture those thoughts in writing and file them so that you can retrieve and use them in the future.

Skill 2

Unleash the Potential of Focused Thinking

"He did each thing as if he did nothing else."
—SPOKEN OF NOVELIST CHARLES DICKENS

What Were They Thinking?

*"An optimist looks at a glass and says the glass is half full.
A pessimist looks at a glass and says it is half empty.
An engineer looks at a glass and says that the glass is
twice as big as it needs to be."*
—SOURCE UNKNOWN

Most people spent lots of time as kids drawing and coloring with crayons. One source says that children in the United States will, on average, wear down 730 crayons by the time they are ten years old.[17] That's a lot of creative energy!

Think back to your childhood. Can you picture the kind of crayons you used? If you really focus you probably will be able even to imagine their *smell*. A Yale University study found that the smell of crayons is among the most recognizable scents to

American adults.[18] You can probably picture the crayons and even the shape and color of the box—a yellow box with green letters. And what's the brand name on that box? In all likelihood, it's "Crayola."

COLOR MY WORLD

Unless you were born under a rock, you probably are familiar with the name Crayola. It is the most popular and recognized crayon brand in the world. Every year, Binney & Smith, the company that makes Crayola products, manufactures nearly 3 billion crayons, at a rate of 12 million a day. That's enough crayons to circle the globe six times![19]

The company was founded by Joseph Binney in 1864 as the Peekskill Chemical Works. In 1885, the founder's son, Edwin, and his cousin, C. Harold Smith, became partners and changed the company's name to Binney & Smith. Up to the turn of the century, the company focused on producing items such as red pigments for barn paint and carbon black used in making lamp black or automobile tires. And their primary method of product development? Simple: ask their customers about their needs and then develop products to meet those needs.

In 1900, the company began making slate pencils for the educational market, and it found that teachers seemed happy to tell company representatives what they desired. When teachers complained about poor chalk, Binney & Smith produced a superior, dustless variety. When they complained that they couldn't buy a decent American crayon (the best were imported from Europe and very expensive), it developed the Crayola. The company introduced the product to the market in 1903 as a box of eight colors that cost a nickel.[20]

Once the company found its niche in the children's market, it became incredibly focused. For a hundred years, it has manufactured superior art supplies for children. Today it dominates that market—even in the face of the electronic revolution. In *The Five Faces of Genius*, Annette Moser-Wellman assessed the company by saying,

> The biggest threat to Crayola's business has been the entry of computer games for kids. Instead of drawing and coloring, kids are tempted by interactive CDs and more. Instead of trying to dominate computer games, Crayola has chosen to flourish within their limitations. They do children's art products better than anyone.[21]

Binney & Smith could have lost focus in an attempt to chase new markets and diversify itself. That's what toy manufacturer Coleco did. The company started out in leather goods in the 1950s and then switched to plastics. In the late 1960s, it was the world's largest manufacturer of above-ground swimming pools. It had found its niche. Yet in the 1970s and 1980s, it chased after the computer game market and then low-end computers. (You may remember ColecoVision.) Then it tried to capitalize on Cabbage Patch dolls. This ultimately drove the company into bankruptcy.[22]

It would have been easy for Binney & Smith to chase after other successes, but it didn't do that. The company has remained focused. And as long as it does, it will continue to excel and to sell more crayons and children's art supplies than any other company in the world.

WHY YOU SHOULD UNLEASH THE POTENTIAL OF FOCUSED THINKING

Focus is just as important in developing ideas for an individual as it is in developing products for a company. Focused thinking can do several things for you:

1. Focused Thinking Harnesses Energy Toward a Desired Goal

In his book, *Focus: The Future of Your Company Depends on It*, marketing consultant Al Ries gives a tremendous illustration:

> The sun is a powerful source of energy. Every hour the sun washes the earth with billions of kilowatts of energy. Yet with a hat and some sun-screen, you can bathe in the light of the sun for hours at a time with few ill effects.
>
> A laser is a weak source of energy. A laser takes a few watts of energy and focuses them in a coherent stream of light. But with a laser you can drill a hole in a diamond or wipe out a cancer.[23]

Focus can bring energy and power to almost anything, whether physical or mental. If you're learning how to pitch a baseball and you want to develop a good curveball, then focused thinking while practicing will improve your technique. If you need to refine the manufacturing process of your product, focused thinking will help you develop the best method. If you want to solve a difficult mathematics problem, focused thinking helps you break through to the solution. That's why philosopher Bertrand Russell asserted, "To be

> "To be able to concentrate for a considerable time is essential to difficult achievement."
> —Bertrand Russell

able to concentrate for a considerable time is essential to difficult achievement." The greater the difficulty of a problem or issue, the more focused thinking time is necessary to solve it.

2. Focused Thinking Gives Ideas Time to Develop

I love to discover and develop ideas. I often bring my creative team together for brainstorming and creative thinking. When we first get together, we try to be exhaustive in our thinking in order to generate as many ideas as possible. The birthing of a potential breakthrough often results from sharing many good ideas.

But to take ideas to the next level, you must shift from being expansive in your thinking to being selective. I

> A good idea can become a great idea when it is given focus time.

have discovered that a good idea can become a great idea when it is given focus time. It's true that focusing on a single idea for a long time can be very frustrating. I've often spent days focusing on a thought and trying to develop it, only to find that I could not improve the idea. But sometimes my perseverance in focused thinking pays off. That brings me great joy. And when focused thinking is at its best, not only does the idea grow, but so do I!

3. Focused Thinking Brings Clarity to the Target

Sociologist Robert Lynd observed that "knowledge is power only if a man knows what facts are not to bother about." Focused thinking removes distractions and mental clutter so that you can concentrate on an issue and think with clarity. That's crucial, because if you don't know what the target is, how will you ever hit it?

I consider golf one of my favorite hobbies. It's a wonderfully challenging game. I like it because the objectives are so clear. Professor William Mobley of the University of South Carolina made the following observation about golf:

> One of the most important things about golf is the presence of clear goals. You see the pins, you know the par—it's neither too easy nor unattainable, you know your average score, and there are competitive goals—competitive with par, with yourself and others. These goals give you something to shoot at. In work, as in golf, goals motivate.

One time on the golf course, I followed a golfer who neglected to put the pin back in the hole after he putted. Because I could not see my target, I couldn't focus properly. My focus quickly turned to frustration—and to poor play. To be a good golfer, a person needs to focus on a clear target. The same is true in thinking. Focus helps you to know the goal—and to achieve it.

4. *Focused Thinking Will Take You to the Next Level*

No one achieves greatness by becoming a generalist. You don't hone a skill by diluting your attention to its development. The only way to get to the next level is to focus. No matter whether your goal is to increase your level of play, sharpen your business plan, improve your bottom line, develop your subordinates, or solve personal problems, you need to focus. Author Harry A. Overstreet observed, "The immature mind hops from one thing to another; the mature mind seeks to follow through."

In *The Road Less Traveled*, M. Scott Peck includes a telling story about himself and his personal ineptitude in fixing things.

Any time he attempted to make minor repairs or put anything together, the result was always confusion, failure, and frustration. Then one day on a walk, he saw a neighbor repairing a lawn

> "The immature mind hops from one thing to another; the mature mind seeks to follow through."
> —Harry A. Overstreet

mower. Peck told the man, "Boy, I sure admire you. I've never been able to fix those kind of things or do anything like that."

"That's because you don't take the time," the neighbor answered. After reflecting on the man's statement, Peck decided to test its truth. The next time he faced a mechanical challenge, he took his time and focused his attention on the problem. Much to his surprise, at age thirty-seven, he succeeded.

After that, he knew that he was not "cursed or genetically defective or otherwise incapacitated or impotent." If he wanted to go to the next level in that area of his life, he could do it—if he was willing to focus on it. He now makes a conscious choice to neglect unimportant things and to focus his attention on his profession: psychiatry.[24]

WHERE SHOULD YOU FOCUS YOUR THINKING?

Peck's realization that he could achieve something that he long thought impossible brings up an important point. Where should you focus your thinking? Does every area of your life deserve dedicated, focused thinking time? Of course, the answer is no.

Be selective, not exhaustive, in your focused thinking. For me, that means dedicating in-depth thinking time to four areas: leadership, creativity, communication, and intentional networking. Your choices will probably differ from mine. Here are a few suggestions to help you figure them out:

Identify Your Priorities

First, take into account your priorities—for yourself, your family, and your team. Author, consultant, and award-winning thinker Edward DeBono quipped, "A conclusion is the place where you get tired of thinking." Unfortunately, many people land on

> "A conclusion is the place where you get tired of thinking."
> —Edward DeBono

priorities based on where they run out of steam. You certainly don't want to do that. Nor do you want to let others set your agenda.

There are many ways to determine priorities. If you know yourself well, begin by focusing on your strengths, the things that make best use of your skills and God-given talents. You might also focus on what brings the highest return and reward. Do what you enjoy most and do best. You could use the 80/20 rule. Give 80 percent of your effort to the top 20 percent (most important) activities. Another way is to focus on exceptional opportunities that promise a huge return. It comes down to this: give your attention to the areas that bear fruit.

Discover Your Gifts

Not all people are self-aware and have a good handle on their own skills, gifts, and talents. They are a little like the comic strip character Charlie Brown. One day after striking out in a baseball game, he says, "Rats! I'll never be a big-league player. I just don't have it! All my life I've dreamed of playing in the big leagues, but I'll never make it."

To which Lucy replies, "Charlie Brown, you're thinking too far ahead. What you need to do is set more immediate goals for yourself."

For a moment, Charlie Brown sees a ray of hope. "Immediate goals?" he says.

"Yes," answers Lucy. "Start with the next inning. When you go out to pitch, see if you can walk out to the mound without falling down!"

I've met many individuals who grew up in a household full of Lucys. They received little encouragement or affirmation, and as a result seem at a loss for direction. If you have that kind of background, you need to work extra hard to figure out what your gifts are. Take a personality profile such as DISC or Myers-Briggs. Interview positive friends and family members to see where they think you shine. Spend some time reflecting on past successes. If you're going to focus your thinking in your areas of strength, you need to know what they are.

Develop Your Dream

One wag said, "Too many minds are like plankton, a small sea plant that goes wherever the current takes it." If you want to achieve great things, you need to have a great dream. James Allen observed, "You will become as small as your controlling desire, as great as your dominant aspiration." If you're not sure of your dream, use your focused thinking time to help you discover it. If your thinking has returned to a particular area time after time, you may be able to discover your dream there. Give it more focused time and see what happens. Once you find your dream, move forward without second-guessing. Take the advice of Satchel Paige: "Don't look back—something might be gaining on you."

The younger you are, the more likely you will give your attention to many things. That's good because if you're

> "You will become as small as your controlling desire, as great as your dominant aspiration."
> —James Allen

young you're still getting to know yourself, your strengths and weaknesses. If you focus your thinking on only one thing and your aspirations change, then you've wasted your best mental energy. As you get older and more experienced, the need to focus becomes more critical. The farther and higher you go, the more focused you can be—and need to be.

How Can You Stay Focused?

Once you have a handle on what you should think about, you must decide how to better focus on it. Here are five suggestions to help you with the process:

1. Remove Distractions

In an article called "Good to Great," author Jim Collins remarked, "The real path to greatness, it turns out, requires simplicity and diligence. It requires clarity, not instant illumination. It demands each of us to focus on what is vital—and to eliminate all of the extraneous distractions."[25] Removing distractions is no small matter in our current culture, but it's critical because, as author and positive mental attitude advocate W. Clement Stone says, you can "keep your mind off the things you don't want by keeping it on the things you do want."

> "Keep your mind off the things you don't want by keeping it on the things you do want."
> —W. Clement Stone

How do you do it? First, by maintaining the discipline of practicing your priorities. Don't do easy things first or hard things first or urgent things first. Do first things first—the activities that give you the highest return. In that way, you keep the distractions to a minimum.

Second, insulate yourself from distractions. I've found that I need blocks of time to think without interruptions. I've mastered the art of making myself unavailable when necessary and going off to my "thinking place" so that I can work without interruptions. Because of my responsibilities as founder of three companies, however, I am always aware of the tension between my need to remain accessible to others as a leader and my need to withdraw from them to think.

The best way to resolve the tension is to understand the value of both activities. Walking slowly through the crowd allows me to connect with people and know their needs. Withdrawing from the crowd allows me to think of ways to add value to them.

My advice to you is to place value on and give attention to both. If you naturally withdraw,

| Wherever you are . . . be there! |

then make sure to get out among people more often. If you're always on the go and rarely withdraw for thinking time, then remove yourself periodically so that you can unleash the potential of focused thinking. And wherever you are . . . be there!

2. Make Time for Focused Thinking

Once you have a place to think, you need the *time* to think. Because of the fast pace of our culture, people tend to multitask. But that's not always a good idea. Switching from task to task can cost you up to 40 percent efficiency. According to researchers, "If you're trying to accomplish many things at the same time, you'll get more done by focusing on one task at a time, *not* by switching constantly from one task to another."[26]

Years ago I realized that my best thinking time occurs in the morning. Whenever possible, I reserve my mornings for thinking and writing. One way to gain time for focused thinking is to impose upon yourself a rule that one company implemented. Don't allow yourself to look at e-mail until after 10 A.M. Instead, focus your energies on your number one priority. Put non-productive time wasters on hold so that you can create thinking time for yourself.

3. Keep Items of Focus Before You

Ralph Waldo Emerson, the great transcendental thinker, believed, "Concentration is the secret of strength in politics, in war, in trade, in short in all management of human affairs." To help me concentrate on the things that matter, I work to keep important items before me. One way is to ask my assistant, Linda Eggers, to keep high priorities in front of me. If an item needs attention or a decision, yet has not landed, I ask her to keep bringing it up, asking me about it, giving me additional information in reference to it.

> "Concentration is the secret of strength in politics, in war, in trade, in short in all management of human affairs."
> —Ralph Waldo Emerson

I also keep items of focus before me in other ways. If I'm working on a presentation or the outline for a book, I'll keep a file or a page on my desk so that I see it every day as I work. That strategy has successfully helped me for thirty years to stimulate and sharpen ideas. If you've never done it, I recommend that you try it. (I'll tell you more about it in the section on reflective thinking.)

4. Set Goals

As a kid, I didn't have any goals. I just wanted to have a good time and play ball. It wasn't until college that I became more focused. At that time I also set my first goals. It was good that

I finally was becoming more intentional about my life, but when I look back at those goals, I laugh. My lifetime goals were so small! If I had worked only until I achieved those goals, I would not have gone far in life.

I believe goals are important. The mind will not focus until it has clear objectives. But the purpose of goals is to focus your attention and give you direction, not to identify a final destination. As you think about your goals, note that they should be

- Clear enough to be kept in focus
- Close enough to be achieved
- Helpful enough to change lives

Those guidelines will get you going. And be sure to write down your goals. If they're not written, I can almost guarantee that they're not focused enough. And if you *really* want to make sure they're focused, take the advice of David Belasco, who says, "If you can't write your idea on the back of my business card, you don't have a clear idea."

Even if you look back years from now and think your goals were too small, they will have served their purpose—if they provide you with direction.

> "If you can't write your idea on the back of my business card, you don't have a clear idea."
> —David Belasco

5. Question Your Progress

Take a good look at yourself from time to time to see whether you are actually making progress. That is the most accurate measure of whether you are making the best use of focused thinking. Ask yourself, "Am I seeing a return for my investment of focused thinking time? Is what I am doing getting me closer to my goals? Am I headed in a direction that helps me to fulfill my commitments, maintain my priorities, and realize my dreams?"

What Are You Giving Up to Go Up?

No one can go to the highest level and remain a generalist. My dad used to say, "Find the one thing you do well and don't do

> To do well at a few things, give up many things.

anything else." I've found that to do well at a few things, I have had to give up many things. As I worked on this chapter, I spent some time reflecting on the kinds of things I've given up. Here are the main ones:

I Can't Know Everyone

I love people, and I'm outgoing. Put me into a room full of people, and I feel energized. So it goes against my grain to restrict myself from spending time with lots of people. To compensate for that, I've done a couple of things. First, I've chosen a strong inner circle of people. They not only provide tremendous professional help, but they also make life's journey much more pleasant. Second, I ask certain friends to catch me up on what's happening in the lives of other friends. I usually do that when I'm traveling and can't block out the time I would need for focused thinking. My main man is Stan Toler, whom I call Mister Relationship. He and I have been friends for over thirty-five years. We have a lot of shared experiences and common friends. One call to Stan is worth a month of socializing. He seems to know what's going on with everybody. He even knows what's happening with me before I do! Recently he faxed me a congratulatory note on the ranking of my latest book, and I didn't have a clue about it.

When I want to know the latest on others—or on me—I call Stan.

I Can't Do Everything

There are only a few exceptional opportunities in any person's lifetime. That's why I strive for excellence in a few things rather than a good performance in many. That's cost me. For example, though I enjoy reading for pleasure, I've not read one novel since I graduated from college. Instead, I've chosen to dedicate my reading time to nonfiction because I believe those works spur the kind of growth I desire both personally and professionally. I'm also utterly helpless when it comes to anything technical. For years, if anything needed to be repaired, I called a friend to help out. Today, I call my son, Joel. If it's mechanical or electronic, he can build it or fix it.

Because of my workload, I also have to skip doing many things that I would love to do. For example, every week I hand off projects that I think would be fun to do myself. I practice the 10-80-10 principle with the people to whom I'm delegating a task. I help with the first 10 percent by casting vision, laying down parameters, providing resources, and giving encouragement. Then once they've done the middle 80 percent, I come alongside them again and help them take whatever it is the rest of the way, if I can. I call it putting the cherry on top.

I Can't Go Everywhere

Every conference speaker and author has to travel a lot. Before I began doing much speaking, that seemed like a glamorous life. But after logging several million miles on airplanes, eating bad food, sleeping in less than comfortable accommodations, keeping a ridiculously demanding schedule, and spending more nights than I can count away from my family, I know what kind of a toll it can take.

Ironically, I still love traveling for pleasure with my wife, Margaret. It's one of our great joys. She and I could take ten vacations a year and enjoy every one of them. Yet we can't, because so much of my time is consumed doing what I was called to do: help people to grow personally and to develop as leaders.

I Can't Be Well-Rounded

Being focused also keeps me from being well-rounded. I tell people, "Ninety-nine percent of everything in life I don't need to know about." I try to focus on the one percent that gives the highest return. And of the remaining ninety-nine, Margaret keeps me aware of whatever I need to know. It's one of the ways I keep from getting totally out of balance in my life.

GETTING A KICK OUT OF IT

Being willing to give up some of the things you love in order to focus on what has the greatest impact isn't an easy lesson to learn. But the earlier you embrace it, the sooner you can dedicate yourself to excellence in what matters most.

> Being willing to give up some of the things you love in order to focus on what has the greatest impact isn't an easy lesson to learn.

I recently read an article about someone who learned that lesson early. Her name is Ashley Martin. On August 30, 2000, she was the first woman to play and score in a Division I college football game. Ashley was the backup kicker on the Jacksonville State (Alabama) football team.

Ashley always has been a good athlete. As a high school freshman in Sharpsburg, Georgia, she lettered in five sports: soccer, basketball, softball, track and football (where she scored 85 points kicking for her team). Her best sport was soccer. How good was she? She was named her team's MVP as a *freshman*. That skill got her an offer of a full soccer scholarship to Jacksonville State.

She got the opportunity to play college football at the school when the football coach, Jack Crowe, saw her kicking field goals for fun after soccer practice. He needed another kicker, so he invited her to try out. She successfully kicked 20 out of 22 extra point attempts and won the job.[27]

But following the 2001 season, Ashley announced that she was done playing football, even though she loved it and wanted to keep playing. Why? Because soccer was more important. Her soccer coach, Lisa Howe, said, "We talked about some goals she has . . . I think when you prioritize, there is just not enough time and energy to do everything."

Ashley agreed. "It would be good for me to be committed to this one thing and focus and work hard on this one thing," she said. "I think that's what I need to do."[28] Ashley was already the highest scorer on her soccer team. There's no telling how far she will go now that she's decided to focus her attention on just one sport. The same can be true for you—if you learn how to unleash the potential of focused thinking.

THINKING QUESTION

Am I dedicated to removing distractions and mental clutter so that I can concentrate with clarity on the real issue?

Putting Focused Thinking into Action

1. At the end of the last chapter, I asked how well you think about the big picture. Now I want to ask the same question related to focused thinking. On a scale of 1 to 10, with one being scattered and 10 being focused, how well do you focus your thinking?

_____

_____

_____

The lower your number, the more time you need to carve out for focused thinking.

2. Get your calendar and figure out how to schedule thinking time. Ideally, you should schedule some time daily, as well as a good block of time once a week. Remember that to be effective, you must remove yourself from distractions, prevent unwanted interruptions, and be able to focus. Pick the best place and your most productive time of day for your focused thinking time. Then put it on your calendar and treat it as you would any important appointment.

3. Our lives are most affected, for good and bad, by just a few events and decisions. Focused thinking can provide the arena to significantly impact those decisions and events. Determine which decisions currently on your plate are most important, and then dedicate some of your scheduled thinking time to address them.

4. If you don't have goals—or your goals don't align with your dreams—then your focus time will get off track. Dedicate this week's large block of thinking time to considering and writing down your current goals.

_____

_____

_____

Skill 3

Discover the Joy of Creative Thinking

"The joy is in creating, not maintaining."
—VINCE LOMBARDI, NFL HALL OF FAME COACH

What Were They Thinking?

Question: "If you could live forever, would you and why?"
Answer: "I would not live forever, because we should not live forever, because if we were supposed to live forever, then we could live forever, but we cannot live forever, which is why I would not live forever."

—1994 MISS USA PAGEANT CONTESTANT

When I went off to college as an eighteen-year-old, one of my first classes was Psychology 101. I found it interesting. I liked people, and I was intrigued to learn more about what made them tick. The teacher wanted us to learn as much about ourselves as others, so we were constantly taking tests, filling out personality profiles and answering self-assessment question-naires. I vividly remember completing a profile a few weeks into the course that measured various natural talents. I don't recall in what area I recorded my highest score, but I certainly remember my greatest weakness: creativity.

That kind of feedback might not have bothered a lot of others in the class, but it crushed me. Not only did I value creativity and desire it, but I knew I required it in order to pursue my chosen profession. I was studying to go into the ministry. That meant that I would be spending many hours every week of my life writing, and I would speak to an audience at least two or three times a week (sometimes more) for the next four decades. How would you feel if you had to listen to an uncreative person speak every week of your life? It's a pretty grim thought!

PROSPECTING FOR IDEAS

> "Originality is the art of concealing your source."
> —Thomas Edison

What was I going to do? I did not consider changing careers an option. I had committed myself to being a pastor; one does not turn his back on what he believes to be God's work. *If I don't have the innate ability to come up with creative thoughts myself,* I thought, *then I'll mine the creative thoughts of others.* I knew that I could become a collector of thoughts more easily than I could become a creator of thoughts. After all, wasn't it the great inventor Thomas Edison who stated, "Originality is the art of concealing your source"?

Every day during the three and a half decades since then, I have read great books, gathered great thoughts, and filed them away by subject. For years as I've written lessons and books, when I wanted a quote, story, or article on a topic, I needed only look in my files to find several excellent pieces of material that I had filed away for just such an occasion.

That discipline has served me well as a writer and speaker. As writer Rosabeth Moss Kanter says, "To stay ahead, you must have your next idea waiting in the wings." I've never failed to have ideas waiting in the wings, or in my case, waiting in the files. But I also discovered something else. By becoming a person always on the lookout for creative ideas, I learned to become a creative thinker myself.

PURE GOLD

You don't have to be a writer, pastor, or professional speaker to value creativity. Annette Moser-Wellman, author of *The Five Faces of Genius*, asserts, *"The most valuable resource you bring to your work and to your firm is your creativity.* More than what you get done, more than the role you play, more than your title, more than your 'output'—it's your ideas that matter."[29] Creativity is pure gold, no matter what you do for a living.

Despite the importance of a person's ability to think with creativity, few people seem to possess the skill in abundance. Author Skipp Ross describes the problem in his book, *Say Yes to Your Potential.* He writes:

A survey was done to discover the creativity level of individuals at various ages. After all the testing, the statistics indicated that 2 percent of the men and women who were in their forties were highly creative. As they looked at younger people, the results emerged that 2 percent of the thirty-five-year-olds were highly creative; 2 percent of the thirty-year-olds were highly creative. This went on down to each age group until they reached the seven-year-old children. Ten percent of them were highly creative. However, further study showed that 90 percent of the five-year-olds were highly creative. Between the ages of five and seven, 80 percent of us who are highly creative develop an image, a picture, an attitude that we are not creative, and we begin to deny that particular part of our God-given equipment."[30]

> "Every child is an artist. The problem is how to remain an artist once he grows up."
> —Pablo Picasso

I don't know why so many people lose their creativity. But I do know that the change doesn't have to be permanent. Pablo Picasso believed, "Every child is an artist. The problem is how to remain an artist once he grows up."

If you're not as creative as you would like to be, you can change your way of thinking, just as I did. Creative thinking isn't necessarily original thinking. In fact, I think people mythologize original thought. Most often, creative thinking is a composite of other thoughts discovered along the way. Even the great artists, whom we consider highly original, learned from their masters, modeled their work on that of others, and brought together a host of ideas and styles to create their own work. Study art, and you will see threads that run through the work of all artists and artistic movements, connecting them to other artists who went before them.

CHARACTERISTICS OF CREATIVE THINKERS

Do you consider yourself highly creative? If Skipp Ross's research is accurate, you might not. Perhaps you're not even sure what I mean when I ask whether you are a creative thinker. Let me explain a few of my observations. Consider some characteristics that creative thinkers have in common:

Creative Thinkers Value Ideas

Annette Moser-Wellman observes, "Highly creative people are dedicated to ideas. They don't rely on their talent alone; they rely on their discipline. Their imagination is like a second skin. They know how to manipulate it to its fullest."[31] Creativity is about having ideas—lots of them. You will have ideas only if you value ideas.

People most often explore ideas in their own areas of interest. That's what my wife, Margaret, does. She has a great love for design and interior decoration. Often when we're out together looking for antiques or décor items, I am amazed by how quickly she can find exactly what she's looking for. Once I asked her how she does it, and she said, "I know exactly what I'm looking for. I've already seen it in a catalog." Margaret gets dozens of catalogs and magazines, and she regularly reviews them to see new items and trends. Because she values ideas, she always has lots of them.

Creative Thinkers Explore Options

I've yet to meet a creative thinker who didn't love options. Exploring a multitude of possibilities helps to stimulate the imagination, and imagination is crucial to creativity. As Albert Einstein put it, "Imagination is more important than knowledge."

People who know me well will tell you that I place a very high value on options. Why? Because they provide the key to finding the best answer—not the only answer. When team members come to me with a problem, I insist that they also supply three possible ways to solve it. Anyone can point out a problem; only people who think well can present possible solutions. Good thinkers come up with the best answers. They create back-up plans that provide them with alternatives. They enjoy freedom that others do not possess. And they will influence and lead others.

Creative Thinkers Embrace Ambiguity

> "It is the dull man who is always sure, and the sure man who is always dull."
> —H. L. Mencken

Writer H. L. Mencken said, "It is the dull man who is always sure, and the sure man who is always dull." Creative people don't feel the need to stamp out uncertainty. They see all kinds of inconsistencies and gaps in life, and they often take delight in exploring those gaps—or in using their imagination to fill them in.

Creative Thinkers Celebrate the Offbeat

Creativity, by its very nature, often explores off of the beaten path and goes against the grain. Diplomat and longtime president of Yale University Kingman Brewster said, "There is a correlation between the creative and the screwball. So we must suffer the screwball gladly." To foster creativity in yourself or others, be willing to tolerate a little oddness.

Creative Thinkers Connect the Unconnected

Because creativity utilizes the ideas of others, there's great value in being able to connect one idea to another—especially to seemingly unrelated ideas. Graphic designer Tim Hansen says, "Creativity is especially expressed in the ability to make connections, to make associations, to turn things around and express them in a new way."

Years ago when I began learning how to connect seemingly unconnected thoughts, I realized that it could often create something special. When you were a kid, did you ever play connect the dots? When you first looked at the page, it seemed just a jumble of dots. But whoever created it had done so with a plan. As you connected the dots, the picture the creator had envisioned emerged at the end of your pencil.

It's easy to connect the dots if you know where you're going. Likewise, it's easy to connect ideas when you have a plan.

> The person with a plan, a picture, will go after thoughts that add value to their thinking.

As a young pastor, I disciplined myself to select my sermon topics three months in advance. That allowed me to be on the lookout for illustrations and ideas that would add value to my messages. That's when I discovered that unconnected ideas get connected when you have a plan. And before long, I realized that creative ideas become more creative when you have a plan.

That's true when writing a book, too. For months I worked diligently on the title, thesis, and outline of *Thinking for a Change.* When I completed that phase of the project, I could begin looking intentionally for content for the book. I was also able to communicate effectively with my writing team about what I was looking for, which directed our efforts in finding good material. And it sparked additional ideas. As we worked on the content, it became clear that we needed to add another chapter to help readers by really hammering home the idea of the power of changed thinking.

Creating additional thoughts is like taking a trip in your car. You may know where you are going, but only as you move toward your destination can you see and experience things in a way not possible before you started. Creative thinking works something like this:

Think ➤ Collect ➤ Create ➤ Correct ➤ Connect

Once you begin to think, you are free to collect. You ask yourself, *What material relates to this thought?* Once you have the material, you ask, *What ideas can make the thought better?* That can start to take an idea to the next level. After that, you can correct or refine it by asking, *What changes can make these ideas better?* Finally, you connect the ideas by positioning them in the right context to make the thought complete and powerful. The whole process happens more readily when you have a framework or picture of where you want to go. That frees you to add value to your thinking. If you go to the ideas, soon the ideas will flow to you.

Creative Thinkers Don't Fear Failure

Overcoming failure is a key to success in life. In 2000 I wrote a book based on that belief titled *Failing Forward.* The thesis of the book is that *the difference between average people and achieving people is their perception of and response to failure.* Creativity demands the ability to be unafraid of failure. Edwin Pond says, "An essential aspect of creativity is not being afraid to fail."

Why is that so crucial? Because creativity equals failure. You may be surprised to hear such a statement, but it's true. Charles Frankel asserts that "anxiety is the essential condition of intellectual and artistic creation." Creativity requires a willingness to look stupid. It means getting out on a limb—knowing that the limb often breaks! Creative people know these things and still keep searching for new ideas. They just don't let the ideas that *don't* work prevent them from coming up with more ideas that *do* work.

WHY YOU SHOULD DISCOVER THE
JOY OF CREATIVE THINKING

Creativity can improve a person's quality of life. Here are five specific things creative thinking has the potential to do for you:

1. Creative Thinking Adds Value to Everything

Wouldn't you enjoy a limitless reservoir of ideas that you could draw upon at any time? That's what creative thinking gives you. For that reason, no matter what you are currently able to do, creativity can increase your capabilities.

Creativity is being able to see what everybody else has seen and think what nobody else has thought so that you can do what nobody else has done. Sometimes creative thinking lies along the lines of invention, where you break new ground. Other times it moves along the lines of innovation, which helps you to do old things in a new way. But either way, it's seeing the world through sufficiently new eyes so that new solutions appear. That always adds value.

A Hollywood hairdresser once got a desperate call from a young actress who

> No matter what you are currently able to do, creativity can make you capable of more.

needed her hair done for a big celebrity party. The hairdresser rushed to the woman's home. He took one look at what she was wearing, pulled a piece of matching ribbon from his travel case, and immediately went to work. In thirty minutes, using nothing but a brush and the ribbon, he had created a masterpiece.

When he turned the young woman around so that she could see herself in the mirror, she said, "Oh, it's gorgeous. Thank you! What do I owe you?"

"Three thousand dollars," the hairdresser replied.

"What!" she cried. "I'm not paying $3,000 for a piece of ribbon."

They locked eyes, neither of them blinking. "Fine," he finally said. And with that, he pulled the ribbon from her hair and they both watched her locks fall into an unruly mess. Handing it to her, he said, "The ribbon is free."

2. Creative Thinking Compounds

Twenty-five years ago, I became passionate about writing books that would add value to people. With great zeal, I started working on my first book. Then the cold water of reality began to douse my flames of passion. I discovered that writing was difficult. For a year, I struggled to write a book of only 100 pages! It turned out to be a small book because I ran out of things to say.

I didn't give up writing because of that difficult experience. I stuck with it and kept working on becoming more creative. Today I have written more than 30 books. And I have at least seven more that I want to write. A young would-be author recently asked me, "How do you write thirty books?" My answer was simple: one word at a time. Over the years, I've found that

Creative Thinking Is Hard Work

but

Creative Thinking Compounds Given Enough
Time and Focus

Perhaps more than any other kind of thinking, creative thinking builds on itself and increases the creativity of the thinker. Poet Maya Angelou observed, "You can't use up creativity. The more you use, the more you have. Sadly, too often creativity is smothered rather than nurtured. There has to be a climate in which new ways of thinking, per-

> "You can't use up creativity. The more you use, the more you have."
> —Maya Angelou

ceiving, questioning are encouraged." If you cultivate creative thinking in an environment that nurtures creativity, there's no telling what kind of ideas you can come up with. (I'll talk more on that later.)

3. Creative Thinking Draws People to You and Your Ideas

Why do people continue to be fascinated by Leonardo da Vinci? Do a quick search of his name on Amazon.com, and you will come up with more than 300 book titles about him—even though he has been dead for nearly 500 years! Why? Because creativity is magnetic.

Creativity is intelligence having fun. People admire intelligence, and they are always attracted to fun—so the combination is fantastic. If anyone could be said to have fun with his intelligence, it was Da Vinci. The diversity of his ideas and expertise staggers the mind. He was a painter, architect, sculptor, anatomist, musician, inventor, and engineer. The term *Renaissance man* was coined because of him.

Just as people were drawn to Da Vinci and his ideas during the Renaissance, they are drawn to creative people today. If you cultivate creativity, you will become more attractive to other people, and they will be drawn to you.

4. Creative Thinking Helps You Learn More

Author and creativity expert Ernie Zelinski says, "Creativity is the joy of not knowing it all. The joy of not knowing it all refers

"Creativity is the joy of not knowing it all."
—Ernie Zelinski

to the realization that we seldom if ever have all the answers; we always have the ability to generate more solutions to just about any problem. Being creative is being able to see or imagine a great deal of opportunity to life's problems. Creativity is having options."[32]

It almost seems too obvious to say, but if you are always actively seeking new ideas, you will learn. Creativity is teachability. It's seeing more solutions than problems. And the greater the quantity of thoughts, the greater the chance for learning something new.

5. Creative Thinking Challenges the Status Quo

Someone said, "Remember that the great wise men of the past held no respect for today's conventions, and neither will the great men of the future."[33] If you desire to improve your world—or even your own situation—then creativity will help you. The *status quo* and creativity are incompatible. Creativity and innovation always walk hand in hand.

When singer Elvis Presley died, he left everything in a trust for Lisa Marie, his young daughter. Soon, however, his estate was in terrible shape. In 1979, Lisa Marie's mother, Priscilla, became a co-executor of the trust and found that if she didn't do something, and quickly, the estate was on the road to ruin.

During his lifetime, Elvis received less than half of what he earned. Colonel Tom Parker, his manager, had a contract that took 50 percent of everything Elvis made, right off the top. That, and a lifestyle of free spending, meant that Elvis often found himself strapped for cash. Several years before he died, Elvis sold off the rights to most of his recordings to raise money. Consequently, his estate receives no royalties from his music, even though Elvis' recordings earned more revenue for RCA than any other artist—even 25 years after his death. Add to that a huge inheritance tax imposed by the government, and an empty mansion, Graceland, gobbling up money through taxes and upkeep, and you can imagine how bleak the situation looked.

Priscilla Presley was not about to allow her daughter's inheritance to be eaten away—but how do you earn income from Elvis' estate without Elvis? Whenever he needed money, he would simply perform at another concert, make another album, or appear in another movie. Priscilla started to think creatively. First, she took the little remaining cash from the estate and invested it into Graceland. Rather than selling it, she opened it to the public as a tourist attraction. It was a great risk, but it paid off. Just thirty-eight days after it opened in 1982, it earned back its investment.

Next, she severed ties with Tom Parker so that 50 percent of the estate's earnings would not continue being funneled to him. Finally, Priscilla began to treat Elvis as a brand. She even promoted legislation in Tennessee to make his likeness intellectual property, which would belong to his estate.[34]

By using creative thinking, Priscilla Presley turned what looked like an impossible situation into a business empire that earns tens of millions of dollars each year. People speculate that Lisa Marie Presley's net worth today exceeds $250 million. Without the creative thinking that shattered the status quo, it likely would have been nothing.

HOW TO DISCOVER THE JOY OF CREATIVE THINKING

At this point you may be saying, "Okay, I'm convinced that creative thinking is important. But how do I find the creativity within me? How do I discover the joy of creative thought?" Here are five ways to do it:

1. Remove Creativity Killers

Economics professor and humor author Stephen Leacock said, "Personally, I would sooner have written *Alice in Wonderland* than the whole *Encyclopedia Britannica*." He valued the warmth of creativity over cold facts. If you do too, then you need to eliminate attitudes that devalue creative thinking.

Take a look at the following phrases. They are almost guaranteed to kill creative thinking any time you hear (or think) them:

- I'm Not a Creative Person
- Follow the Rules
- Don't Ask Questions
- Don't Be Different
- Stay Within the Lines
- There Is Only One Way
- Don't Be Foolish
- Be Practical
- Be Serious
- Think of Your Image
- That's Not Logical
- It's Not Practical
- It's Never Been Done
- It Can't Be Done
- It Didn't Work for Them
- We Tried That Before
- It's Too Much Work
- We Can't Afford to Make a Mistake
- It Will Be Too Hard to Administer

- We Don't Have the Time
- We Don't Have the Money
- Yes, But . . .
- Play Is Frivolous
- Failure Is Final

If you think you have a great idea, don't let anyone talk you out of it even if it sounds foolish. Don't let yourself or anyone else subject you to creativity killers. After all, you can't do something new and exciting if you force yourself to stay in the same old rut. Or as Edward De Bono observed in *New Think*, "You cannot dig a hole in a different place by digging the same hole deeper." Don't just work harder at the same old thing. Make a change.

2. Think Creatively by Asking the Right Questions

Creativity is largely a matter of asking the right questions. Management trainer Sir Antony Jay said, "The uncreative mind can spot wrong answers, but it takes a creative mind to spot wrong questions." Wrong questions shut down the process of creative thinking. They direct thinkers down the same *old* path, or they chide them into believing that thinking isn't necessary at all.

> "The uncreative mind can spot wrong answers, but it takes a creative mind to spot wrong questions."
> —Antony Jay

To stimulate creative thinking, ask yourself questions such as . . .

- Why must it be done *this* way?
- What is the root problem?
- What are the underlying issues?

- What does this remind me of?
- What is the opposite?
- What metaphor or symbol helps to explain it?
- Why is it important?
- What's the *hardest* or *most expensive* way to do it?
- Who has a different perspective on this?
- What happens if we *don't* do it at all?

You get the idea—and you can probably come up with better questions yourself. Physicist Tom Hirschfield observed, "If you don't ask, 'Why this?' often enough, somebody will ask, 'Why you?'" If you want to think creatively, you must ask good questions. You must challenge the process.

3. Develop a Creative Environment

Charlie Brower said, "A new idea is delicate. It can be killed by a sneer or a yawn; it can be stabbed to death by a quip and worried to death by a frown on the right man's brow." Negative environments kill thousands of great ideas every minute.

A creative environment, on the other hand, becomes like a greenhouse where ideas get seeded, sprout up, and flourish. A creative environment:

- *Encourages Creativity:* David Hills says, "Studies of creativity suggest that the biggest single variable of whether or not employees will be creative is whether they perceive they have permission." When innovation and good thinking are openly encouraged and rewarded, then people see that they have permission to be creative. At the INJOY Group, I encourage creativity by regularly calling creative team sessions where thinkers gather to come up with new and better ideas. With the right people in the room, three things always happen: the ideas always get raised to a higher level; the energy and synergy gets raised to a higher level; and the companies get raised to a higher level.

- *Places a High Value on Trust among Team Members and Individuality:* Creativity always risks failure. That's why trust is so important to creative people. Mystery writer Rita Mae Brown observes, "Creativity comes from trust. Trust your instincts. And never hope more than you work." In the creative process, trust comes from the fact that the people working together want what's best for the organization and each other. It comes from knowing that people on the team have experience launching successful, creative ideas. And it comes from the assurance that the time coming up with creative ideas won't go to waste, because the ideas will be implemented.

> "Creativity comes from trust. Trust your instincts. And never hope more than you work."
> —Rita Mae Brown

- *Embraces Those Who Are Creative:* Creative people celebrate the offbeat. Admittedly, they are sometimes off center. How should creative people be treated? I take the advice of Tom Peters: "Weed out the dullards—nurture the nuts!" I do that by spending time with them, which I enjoy anyway. I especially like to pull people into brainstorming sessions. People look forward to an invitation to such meetings because the time will be filled with energy, ideas, and laughter. And the odds are high that a new project, seminar, or business strategy will result. When that happens, they also know a party's coming!

- *Focuses on Innovation, Not Just Invention:* Creativity needs to begin somewhere. Sam Weston, creator of the popular action figure GI Joe, said, "Truly groundbreaking ideas are rare, but you don't necessarily need one to make a career out of creativity. My definition of creativity is the logical combination of two or more existing elements that result in a new concept. The best way to make a living with your imagination is to develop innovative applications, not imagine completely new concepts."

Creative people say, "Give me a good idea and I'll give you a better idea!" Fortunately, I learned this lesson early. Seldom do I have an original idea. Often I take an idea that someone else gives me and raise it to a higher level. That has been my approach to creativity. When I speak at one of my conferences, I frequently describe the book idea I'm currently working on. Then I invite audience members to share their thoughts, ideas, and illustrations with me to make the book better. I tell them, "I'll take what you give me, make it better, and give you credit." Then I smile and say, "Then I'll sell you the book." We all get a good laugh out of it. I'm happy to receive a good idea; they're happy to receive recognition. (And I send them a free book.)

- *Places a High Value on Options:* A woman listened to her suitor's marriage proposal, then said, "I'm sorry, Fred, but I cannot marry you."

   "Why?" he asked. "Is there someone else?"

   "Oh, Fred," she replied, "there must be!"

Creative people are "other" thinkers. They are always thinking about and looking for other ways of doing things because they know that options bring opportunities. When anyone in my inner circle brings me an item requiring a decision, I ask for three things: the best information possible, possible options, and their reasoning behind the option they would choose. I've found that this kind of optional thinking often produces the best results.

- *Is Willing to Let People Go Outside the Lines:* Most people automatically stay within lines, even if those lines have been arbitrarily drawn or are terribly out of date. Sometimes when I teach about creativity, I challenge the audience with the following exercise:

> *Draw four straight lines through all of the dots without lifting your pen.*

This problem can be solved only if a person is willing to draw lines out of the box. *(See the end of the chapter for the solution.)* Most people aren't willing to do that. Remember, most limitations we face are not imposed on us by others; we place them on ourselves. Lack of creativity often falls into that category.

If you want to be more creative, challenge boundaries. Inventor Charles Kettering said, "All human development, no matter what form it takes, must be outside the rules; otherwise, we would never have anything new." A creative environment takes that into account.

> "All human development, no matter what form it takes, must be outside the rules; otherwise, we would never have anything new."
> —Charles Kettering

- *Appreciates the Power of a Dream:* A creative environment promotes the freedom of a dream. A creative environment encourages the use of a blank sheet of paper and the question, "If we could draw a picture of what we want to accomplish, what would that look like?" A creative environment allowed Martin Luther King, Jr., to speak with passion and declare to millions, "I have a dream," not "I have a goal." Goals may give focus, but dreams give power. Dreams expand the world. That is why James Allen suggested that "dreamers are the saviors of the world."

The more creativity-friendly you can make your environment, the more potential it has to become creative.

4. Spend Time with Other Creative People

What if the place you work has an environment hostile to creativity, and you possess little ability to change it? One possibility is to change jobs. But what if you desire to keep working there despite the negative environment? Your best option is to find a way to spend time with other creative people.

Creativity is contagious. Have you ever noticed what happens during a good brainstorming session? One person throws out an idea. Another person uses it as a springboard to discover another idea. Someone else takes it in yet another, even better direction. Then somebody grabs hold of it and takes it to a whole new level. The interplay of ideas can be electric.

I have a strong group of creative individuals in my life. I make sure to spend regular time with them. When I leave them, I always feel energized, I'm full of ideas, and I see things differently. They truly are indispensable to my life.

It's a fact that you begin to think like the people you spend a lot of time with. The more time you can spend with creative people engaging in creative activities, the more creative you will become.

5. *Get Out of Your Box*

Actress Katharine Hepburn remarked, "If you obey all the rules . . . you will miss all the fun." While I don't think it's necessary to break *all* the rules (many are in place to protect us), I do think it's unwise to allow self-imposed limitations to hinder us. Creative thinkers are out-of-the-box people. They know that they must repeatedly break out of the "box" of their own history and personal limitations in order to experience creative breakthroughs.

The most effective way to help yourself get out of the box is to expose yourself to new paradigms. One way you can do that is by traveling to new places. Explore other cultures, countries, and traditions. Find out how people very different from you live and think. Another is to read on new subjects. I'm naturally curious and love to learn, but I still have a tendency to read books only on my favorite subjects, such as leadership. I sometimes have to force myself to read books that broaden my thinking, because I know it's worth it. If you want to break out of your own box, get into somebody's else's. Read broadly.

PLAY IS THE WAY

Many people mistakenly believe that if individuals aren't born with creativity, they will never be creative. But you can see from the many strategies and examples I've given that creativity can be cultivated. Some people work so hard to make themselves creative thinkers, and they spend so much time thinking outside of the box, that I'm not sure they even *have* a box anymore.

I recently read an article about a group like that. Its members make up a small marketing company in Richmond, Virginia, called Play. The company is a caldron of creativity: the corner conference room is called the "playroom." Employees invent their own titles, some of which include the person "in charge of what's next," the "voice of reason," "check, please," and "1.21 jigawatts." They are encouraged to take radical sabbaticals to climb mountains, learn to surf, or do anything else that might spur greater creativity.

When the ideas fly and everyone's pushing the envelope, employees call that "mojo." When a team hits a wall and a deadline approaches, they "red flag" a project and *everyone* in the organization pitches in. "No one goes home before the owner of a red-flag project feels comfortable," explains employee Courtney Page, "no matter how long it takes."

LIVE, EAT, BREATHE CREATIVITY

The founders of Play have created an incredible environment of creativity. Bill Howland, product manager of the Center for Creative Leadership, which recently tested Play's ability to foster creativity, said that Play's "scores were off the charts. I have not seen another company with such an open and creative environment in my six years with the center."

The company's values are straightforward: people, play, and profit, in that order. Robb Pair, who leads the company's merchandising division, says, "Working at Play really gives me a feeling of 'no limits.' Risk is encouraged, and I have the chance to explore my potential and abilities."

Play cofounder Andy Sefanovich describes how Play has been able to foster such creativity: "What we're doing," he says, "is building a creative *community*—not mystifying creativity as a special talent of a chosen few."[35]

And what's their advice to people who want to become more creative, as they are? "Look at more stuff, and think about it harder." That's a formula all of us can learn to embrace.

THINKING QUESTION

Am I working to break out of my "box" of limitations so that I explore ideas and options to experience creative breakthroughs?

Putting Creative Thinking into Action

1. If you have been using some method of capturing your ideas in a notebook, computer, or filing system, grab hold of it and look through some of the ideas you've recorded. (If you haven't been capturing your ideas on paper, you're missing an opportunity to take them to the next level. Rather than completing this first exercise, begin capturing ideas on paper for the next 90 days.)

Look through your ideas and find one that you believe has great potential. Now ask yourself the following questions to stretch that idea:

- Why do I like this idea?
- What are the underlying issues involved with it?
- What does this remind me of?
- What is the opposite?
- What metaphor or symbol helps explain it?
- What is the value of the idea?
- What's the *hardest* or *most expensive* way to carry it out?
- Who has a different perspective on this?
- What happens if I *don't* do it at all?
- In my wildest dreams, what can this idea lead to?

I encourage you to add other questions of your own. The idea is to get outside of your box and let your ideas take you anywhere they want you to. The only rules are 1) you're not allowed to shut down your thinking process with self-editing, criticism, or other creativity killers; and 2) You must try to capture as many of your ideas as possible on paper.

2. Think about your working environment. Does it naturally foster creativity or tend to shut it down? If it promotes creative thought, count your blessings and thank your colleagues and boss. If it doesn't, figure out if you can make it friendlier to creativity. If you're the boss, then changing the culture is your responsibility. Praise and reward creative thinking and innovation. Introduce play. Give people time to recharge their mental batteries, similar to Play's radical sabbaticals. Hire a consultant to teach people how to think out of the box. Do whatever's necessary.

3. If you have the resources to go to another country where you can immerse yourself in a different culture, you may want to plan your next vacation around it. If you don't, then plan to read three books that take you out of your area of expertise. Don't pick something that will bore you or that will go way over your head. Just expose yourself to something that makes you stretch your mind.

Solution to exercise for Thinking Outside the Lines:

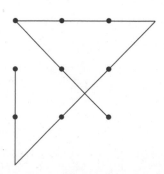

Skill 4

Recognize the Importance of Realistic Thinking

"The first responsibility of a leader is to define reality."
—MAX DEPREE, Chairman of the Board
of Herman Miller, Inc.

What Were They Thinking?

*"The police are not here to create disorder.
They're here to preserve disorder."*
—MAYOR RICHARD DALEY, during 1968 Democratic
National Convention in Chicago

One of the conferences I've especially enjoyed hosting recently is called "Reality Leadership." It's an intense one-day conference that focuses on four of the most difficult challenges facing any leader: influencing change, resolving conflict, developing leaders, and making the tough call. I love that conference because it highlights real-life case studies of leaders who have successfully faced those tasks themselves, and it helps people deal with real problems. As anyone knows who's been out of school for a few years, there's usually a huge gap between a college education and the reality of the working world.

After one conference, I hosted a roundtable discussion. As I outlined some developing trends, I could tell that many in the group didn't like what they were hearing. I could sympathize. When I started my career fresh out of school, I was an idealistic thinker, not a realistic one. Take a look at some of my misconceptions and the realities I faced:

Misconception	Reality
I could make everyone happy.	There will be conflict.
People like change if it's done properly.	People resist change regardless.
It is enough that the leader takes care of the people.	People must be developed to be effective.
Good leadership makes tough calls unnecessary.	Tough calls must always be made.

Honestly, early in my career, I went out of my way to avoid too much realistic thinking because I thought it would interfere with my creative thinking. But as I've grown, I've come to realize that realistic thinking adds to my life.

REALITY CHECK

Reality is the difference between what we wish and what is. I learned that truth slowly, lesson by lesson. In my first year of ministry, I discovered that no matter how hard I worked or what I did, I could not please *everybody*. I made that discovery when I failed to receive a unanimous vote of approval from my people during my first annual congregational meeting.

One by one my misconceptions fell. And in time, I evolved into a more realistic thinker. That process went in phases.

First, I did not engage in realistic thinking at all. After a while, I realized that it was necessary, so I began to engage in it occasionally. (But I didn't like it because I thought it was too negative. And any time I could delegate it, I did.) Eventually, I found that I *had* to engage in realistic thinking if I was going to solve problems and learn from my mistakes. And in time, I became willing to think realistically *before* I got in trouble and make it a continual part of my life. Today, I encourage my key leaders to think realistically. We make realistic thinking the foundation of our business because we derive certainty and security from it.

I continue to grow in the area of realistic thinking, but still it is not an area of natural strength. I have much to learn. I was reminded of that recently by my brother, Larry, who is a very realistic thinker. At a board meeting for EQUIP, the non-profit organization I founded to teach leadership to pastors overseas, we were discussing the budget for the coming year. The tragedy of September 11, 2001, adversely affected the income of most non-profit organizations not involved in the relief effort. Although giving was down for EQUIP, I believed that things would soon turn around and we could adopt a budget similar to the one from the previous year.

Larry, however, who is also a member of EQUIP's board of directors, did not agree. He wanted to be more practical.

"John," he said, "you can't let your natural optimism drive this budget. Let's look at the worst-case scenario. What will EQUIP's income be if things don't turn around? That should be our base for the budget and staffing." We talked about that idea for a while, and Larry concluded by saying, "You've always got to ask yourself, 'What's the worst-case scenario?' That's the only way to keep your organization financially sound." And Larry would know about that. He's an excellent businessperson. Because of his savvy and ability to think realistically, he's built many successful businesses, and he's been financially independent since he was in his early twenties.

WHY YOU SHOULD RECOGNIZE THE IMPORTANCE OF REALISTIC THINKING

If you're a naturally optimistic person, as I am, you may not possess great desire to become a more realistic thinker. But cultivating the ability to be realistic in your thinking will not undermine your faith in people, nor will it lessen your ability to see and seize opportunities. Instead, it will add value to you in other ways:

1. Realistic Thinking Minimizes Downside Risk

Actions always have consequences; realistic thinking helps you to determine what those consequences could be. And that's crucial, because only by recognizing and considering consequences can you plan for them. If you plan for the worst-case scenario, you can minimize the downside risk.

2. Realistic Thinking Gives You a Target and Game Plan

I've known businesspeople who were not realistic thinkers. Here's the good news: they were very positive and had a high degree of hope for their business. Here's the bad news: hope is not a strategy.

Realistic thinking leads to excellence in leadership and management because it requires people to face reality. They begin to define their target and develop a game plan to hit it. When people engage in realistic thinking, they also begin to simplify practices and procedures, which results in better efficiency.

Truthfully, in business only a few decisions are important. Realistic thinkers understand the difference between the important decisions and

> "Until thought is linked with purpose there is no intelligent accomplishment."
> —James Allen

those that are merely necessary in the normal course of business. The decisions that matter relate directly to your purpose. James Allen was right when he wrote, "Until thought is linked with purpose there is no intelligent accomplishment."[36]

3. Realistic Thinking Is a Catalyst for Change

People who rely on hope for their success rarely make change a high priority. If you have only hope, you imply that achievement and success are out of your hands. It's a matter of luck or chance. Why bother changing?

Realistic thinking can dispel that kind of wrong attitude. There's nothing like staring reality in the face to make a person recognize the need for change. Change alone doesn't bring growth but you cannot have growth without change.

4. Realistic Thinking Provides Security

Any time you have thought through the worst that can happen and you have developed

> Disappointment is the difference between expectations and reality.

contingency plans to meet it, you become more confident and secure. It's reassuring to know that you are unlikely to be surprised. Disappointment is the difference between expectations and reality. Realistic thinking minimizes the difference between the two.

5. *Realistic Thinking Gives You Credibility*

Realistic thinking helps people to buy in to the leader and his or her vision. Leaders continually surprised by the unexpected soon lose credibility with their followers. On the other hand, leaders who think realistically and plan accordingly position their organizations to win. That gives their people confidence in them.

The best leaders ask realistic questions *before* casting vision. They ask themselves things like . . .

- Is it possible?
- Does this dream include everyone or just a few?
- Have I identified and articulated the areas that will make this dream difficult to achieve?

I learned a great deal about the credibility that comes from realistic thinking in 1983 when the church I led needed to relocate. We were looking at purchasing 80 acres in east San Diego. The good news was that the property was in a prime location; the bad news was that there were many obstacles to overcome before we could relocate. As any experienced businessperson knows, a multimillion-dollar building project is difficult and complicated, but this one ran up against ridiculous difficulties because of local bureaucracy, environmental regulations, and red tape.

As I presented the vision for our relocation to our people, I chose to communicate the challenges realistically. As we began to raise funds to purchase the property, I had to make sure that everyone understood that the land wasn't currently zoned for our purposes. After we bought the land, the real difficulties began. For eight long years, whenever I communicated the opportunities of the vision, I gave an equal amount of time to the obstacles. It was sometimes painful, but by including realistic thinking in the communication, we were able to sustain the dream over a long period of time.

6. Realistic Thinking Provides a Foundation to Build On

Thomas Edison observed, "The value of a good idea is in using it." The bottom line on realistic thinking is that it helps you to make an idea usable by taking away the "wish" factor. Most ideas and efforts don't accomplish their intended results because they rely too much on what we wish rather than what is.

You can't build a house in midair; it needs a solid foundation. Ideas and plans are the same. They need something concrete on which to build. Realistic thinking provides that solid foundation.

7. Realistic Thinking Is a Friend to Those in Trouble

If creativity is what you would do if you were unafraid of the possibility of failure, then reality is dealing with failure if it does happen. Realistic thinking gives you something concrete to fall back on during times of trouble, which can be very reassuring. Certainty in the midst of uncertainty brings stability.

8. Realistic Thinking Brings the Dream to Fruition

British novelist John Galsworthy wrote, "Idealism increases in direct proportion to one's dis-

> "Idealism increases in direct proportion to one's distance from the problem."
> —John Galsworthy

tance from the problem." If you don't get close enough to a problem, you can't tackle it. If you don't take a realistic look at your dream—and what it will take to accomplish it—you will never achieve it. Realistic thinking helps to pave the way for bringing any dream to fruition.

HOW TO RECOGNIZE THE
IMPORTANCE OF REALISTIC THINKING

Because I'm naturally optimistic rather than realistic, I've had to take concrete steps to improve my thinking in this area. Here are five things I do to improve my realistic thinking:

1. Develop an Appreciation for Truth

I could not develop as a realistic thinker until I gained an appreciation for realistic thinking. And that means learning to look at and enjoy truth. President Harry S. Truman said, "I never give 'em hell. I just tell the truth and they think it is hell." That's the way many people react to truth.

People tend to exaggerate their success and minimize their failures or deficiencies. They live according to Ruckert's Law, believing there is nothing so small that it can't be blown out of proportion. I heard a humorous story that illustrates that ability. The chairman of a local chamber of commerce had to introduce the speaker at the organization's annual black-tie dinner.

"The man who I am about to introduce," he said, "is someone I know you'll enjoy listening to. He is the most gifted businessman in the country. He has made one hundred million dollars in California oil."

The speaker, embarrassed, came to the podium. "Thank you

for your kind introduction, Mr. Chairman," he said. "However, the facts need some clarification. It wasn't oil; it was coal. It wasn't California; it was Pennsylvania. It wasn't one hundred million; it was one hundred thousand. It wasn't me; it was my brother. And he didn't make it; he lost it."

Another not-so-humorous illustration concerning the truth surfaced in 2001. If you follow college football, you are probably aware of what happened to coach George O'Leary. The former Georgia Tech football coach received and accepted an offer for what he called his dream job—head coach for the University of Notre Dame. But O'Leary had a problem. Years before, he had created a resume that didn't match the reality of his experience. His resume claimed that he had a degree which he hadn't earned, and it invented college playing experience that he didn't possess. When officials at Notre Dame discovered the discrepancy, O'Leary lost his credibility—and his dream job.

"Due to a selfish and thoughtless act many years ago," O'Leary said, "I have personally embarrassed Notre Dame, its alumni and fans. The integrity and credibility of Notre Dame is impeccable and with that in mind, I will resign my position as head football coach."

Notre Dame athletic director Kevin White commented, "I understand that these inaccuracies represent a very human failing;

> "Men occasionally stumble over the truth, but most pick themselves up and hurry off as if nothing has happened."
> —Winston Churchill

nonetheless, they constitute a breach of trust that makes it impossible for us to go forward with our relationship."[37]

Unfortunately, many people today could be described by a quote from Winston Churchill: "Men occasionally stumble over the truth, but most pick themselves up and hurry off as if

> The truth will set you free—but first it will make you angry!

nothing has happened." More recently, television journalist Ted Koppel observed, "Our society finds truth too strong a medicine to digest undiluted. In its purest form, truth is not a polite tap on the shoulder. It is a howling reproach." In other words, the truth will set you free—but first it will make you angry! If you want to become a realistic thinker, however, you need to get comfortable dealing with the truth and face up to it.

2. Do Your Homework

A college recruiter heard good things about a high school basketball player from a small town. He got to the town too late for the game, but was able to meet the young man and his coach. The recruiter said to the young man, "I hear you're pretty good."

"The best there is," the player replied. "I average 45 points per game. I am the best rebounder in my school. And I've led our team to three undefeated seasons and three state championships."

After talking to the player, the recruiter said to the coach, "What a talent! So tell me, does he have any weaknesses?"

"Well," the coach said sheepishly, "He does have a tendency to exaggerate."

The process of realistic thinking begins with doing your homework. You must first get the facts. Former governor, congressman, and ambassador Chester Bowles said, "When you approach a problem, strip yourself of preconceived opinions and prejudice, assemble and learn the facts of the situation, make the decision which seems to you to be the most honest, and then stick to it." It doesn't matter how sound your thinking is if it's based on faulty data or assumptions. You can't think well in the absence of facts (or in the presence of poor information).

You can also find out what others have done in similar circumstances. Remember, your thinking doesn't necessarily

> Some of my best thinking has been done by others!

have to be original; it just has to be solid. Why not learn all that you can from good thinkers who have faced similar situations in the past? Some of my best thinking has been done by others!

3. Think Through the Pros and Cons

There's nothing like taking the time to really examine the pros and cons of an issue to give you a strong dose of reality. It rarely comes down to simply choosing the course of action with the greatest number of pros, because all pros and cons do not carry equal weight. But that's not the value of the exercise, anyway. Rather, it helps you to dig into the facts, examine an issue from many angles, and really count the cost of a possible course of action.

4. Picture the Worst-Case Scenario

The essence of realistic thinking is discovering, picturing, and examining the worst-case scenario. Ask yourself questions such as,

- What if sales fall short of projections?
- What if revenue hits rock bottom? (Not an optimist's rock bottom, but *real* rock bottom!)
- What if we don't win the account?
- What if the client doesn't pay us?
- What if we have to do the job short-handed?
- What if our best player gets sick?
- What if all the colleges reject my application?
- What if the market goes belly up?

- What if the volunteers quit?
- What if nobody shows up?

You get the idea. The point is that you need to think about worst-case possibilities whether you are running a business, leading a department, pastoring a church, coaching a team, or planning your personal finances. Your goal isn't to be negative or to *expect* the worst, just to be ready for it in case it happens. That way, you give yourself the best chance for a positive result—no matter what.

If you picture the worst case and examine it honestly, then you really have experienced a reality check. You're ready for anything. As you do that, take the advice of Charles Hole, who advised, "Deliberate with caution, but act with decision; and yield with graciousness or oppose with firmness."

5. Align Your Thinking with Your Resources

> One of the keys to maximizing realistic thinking is aligning your resources with your objectives.

One of the keys to maximizing realistic thinking is aligning your resources with your objectives. Looking at pros and cons and examining worst-case scenarios will make you aware of any gaps between what you desire and what really is. Once you know what those gaps are, you can use your resources to fill them. After all, that's what resources are for.

SUPER BOWL, SUPER DOME, SUPER SECURITY

Our country received lessons in realistic thinking following the tragedy of September 11, 2001. The destruction of the World

Trade Center buildings in New York City far surpassed any worst-case scenarios that anyone might have envisioned. In the wake of that event, we now find that we don't have the luxury of avoiding or neglecting realistic thinking.

I was reminded of that on Sunday, February 3, 2002, when I attended the Super Bowl in New Orleans, Louisiana. I had been to the big game twice before, to root for the home team—first San Diego and later Atlanta—and had seen both teams lose! But I had never been to a game like this.

The occasion had been designated a National Security Special Event. That meant that the U.S. Secret Service would be overseeing it; military personnel would work with local law enforcement; and security would be of the highest caliber. The Secret Service brought in several hundred agents and secured the area. In preparation for the game, access to the Super Dome was highly restricted, with intensified screening. Officials blocked off roads, closed the nearby interstate, and designated the area a no-fly zone.

We arrived early at the dome—officials suggested fans arrive up to five hours ahead of game time—and we immediately saw evidence of the precautionary measures. Eight-foot fences surrounded the whole area, and concrete barriers prevented unauthorized vehicles from getting close to the building. We could see sharpshooters positioned at various locations, including on the roof of some adjacent buildings. When we reached a gate, police officers and security personnel patted us down and examined everyone's belongings. After that they directed us to go through metal detectors. Only then did they allow us into the stadium.

"That's all well and good," you may be saying, "but what would have happened had there been a terrorist attack?" The Secret Service had that covered too, because they had prepared for the worst-case scenario. Evacuation plans had been put into place, and personnel at the Super Dome had been drilled to make sure everyone knew what to do in case of an emergency.

New Orleans mayor Marc Morial said the day before the Super Bowl, "We want to send a message to all visitors that New Orleans is going to be the safest place in America."[38] We got the message. We didn't feel the least bit worried. That's what happens when leaders recognize the importance of realistic thinking.

THINKING QUESTION

*Am I building a solid mental foundation on
facts so that I can think with certainty?*

Putting Realistic Thinking into Action

1. What is your natural bent? Is it toward optimism or realism? Take a look at the phases I went through in my evolution as a more realistic thinker (plus one more level I have not yet achieved) and see which statement best describes you.

   1. I do not engage in realistic thinking.
   2. I do not like realistic thinking.
   3. I will let someone else do realistic thinking.
   4. I will do realistic thinking only after I am in trouble.
   5. I will do realistic thinking before I am in trouble.
   6. I will continually make realistic thinking part of my life.
   7. I will encourage my key leaders to do the same.
   8. I will make realistic thinking the foundation of our business.
   9. I derive certainty and security from realistic thinking.

10. I rely heavily on facts and often make judgments according to the worst-case scenario.

The lower your number, the more you need to grow.

2. If you haven't highly developed your ability to think realistically, then maybe you need a strong dose of truth. Ask five astute people (friends, coworkers, your spouse, your supervisor, etc.) to talk to you about your three greatest strengths and weaknesses. Ideally, they should write down their observations and explain them to you. As they talk, you are not allowed to defend yourself. You are allowed only to ask questions that help you to understand their observations. Make notes, if necessary.

Take all of the comments you receive, along with your notes, and spend a whole day examining yourself in light of what you were told. Think about how their comments can help you, and how you can improve in your areas of weakness and capitalize on your strengths. The first step in gaining an appreciation for the truth is learning to deal with the truth about yourself.

3. The next time you have a problem to solve or a project to complete, use the guidelines from this chapter to help you cultivate a more realistic view of the issues.

- Do your homework.
- Work through the pros and cons.
- Find the worst-case scenario.
- Align your thinking and your resources.

Go through all four steps before you take action.

Skill 5

Release the Power of Strategic Thinking

*"Most people spend more time planning their
summer vacation than planning their lives."*
—SOURCE UNKNOWN

What Were They Thinking?

*If quitters never win, and winners never quit,
then why should I quit while I'm ahead?*

When you hear the words "strategic thinking," what comes to
mind? Do visions of business plans dance in your head? Do you
conjure up marketing plans, the kind that can turn a company
around? Perhaps you contemplate global politics. Or you recall
some of history's greatest military campaigns: Hannibal
crossing the Alps to surprise the Roman Army, Charlemagne's
conquest of Western Europe, or the Allies' D-Day invasion of
Normandy. Strategic thinking often gets associated with war. In
fact, the formal definition of *strategy* has a strong military bent.
Consider a common dictionary definition:

1. the science of planning and directing large-scale military operations, specifically (as distinguished from tactics)

of maneuvering forces into the most advantageous position prior to actual engagement with the enemy[39]

Even the most basic definition uses a military reference and distinguishes tactics from strategic thinking. (Tactics are actions taken in battle, while strategies are plans prior to it.) But strategy doesn't have to be restricted to military action—or even to business. Strategic thinking can make a positive impact on any area of life. Let me tell you a story that illustrates my point.

A Real Prize Winner

Evelyn Ryan lived in Defiance, Ohio, in the mid-1900s. She never learned to drive, and she never worked outside of the house after she started having children. She lived at a time when a mother was expected to stay at home. That might not have been a problem, except that her family was desperately short of money. In all, she had ten children! And her husband, Kelly, made only a meager living working in a machine shop. To make matters worse, Kelly was an alcoholic who drank up about a third of his take-home pay every week.

Anyone who passed Evelyn Ryan on the street likely would not have identified her as an impressive strategic thinker, yet she was. She had to figure out a way to raise her ten children, take care of the house, and bring in enough extra money for the family to survive.

Evelyn lived at a time when product manufacturers frequently sponsored contests. I was growing up then, so I remember those radio and television announcements inviting people to write in twenty-five words or less why they liked Tide detergent or asking them to finish a jingle for Dr.

Pepper. Today's advertising relies heavily on dramatic images, but advertising in the forties and fifties depended heavily upon slogans. You couldn't drive in the country without passing a series of clever signs advertising Burma Shave. Product manufacturers continually sponsored contests promising prizes or cash awards.

Evelyn had a natural ability with words, which she had cultivated working on the local newspaper before she got married. So she had a logical plan. Since she couldn't go out to work to earn extra money (can you imagine what day care would have cost for ten kids, had it even been available?), she earned money and won things the family needed by entering contests.

PLANNING PAYS

The ability to write hundreds of poems, jingles, and promotional paragraphs, all while managing, feeding, and doing laundry for a family of twelve, required great strategy. Evelyn was up to the task. First, she had elaborate systems for finding and storing contest entry blanks and proofs of purchase, such as box tops and can labels. Second, she had to write while she worked. Each year she bought a new spiral notebook, which she used to capture her thoughts and any information needed to keep track of the various contests she entered. Her next challenge was figuring out *when* to write. She kept her notebook open and nearby as she worked around the house, but she found that ironing provided the best time to write.

Evelyn didn't restrict her strategic thinking to the logistics of writing. She also strategically selected *what* she wrote. She chose very carefully the words for any given contest. Her daughter, Terry, recalled how Evelyn approached the task:

Contesting, as she always said, required more than collecting box tops and being clever. There was *form* to consider (some contests required the use of specific words, or gave points for the use of product-related words in an entry), *product focus* (was it aimed at families, at young men, at children?), and *judges*. The advertising agency hired to judge the contest was always a more important consideration for the entrants than the sponsor or the product. Each agency had its preference for rhyme or prose, for humorous or straight material.[40]

Evelyn learned the likes and dislikes of every ad agency that administered contests, and her strategy served her well. Over the years she won several washers and dryers for her large family, dozens of other large and small appliances, two brand new cars (which they sold), hundreds of small cash awards, and large cash awards of $5,000 and $3,400. She used the first big cash prize as a down payment for a house so that the family of twelve could move out of a two-bedroom rental. She used the other to pay off a second mortgage that her husband had secretly taken out (she didn't find out about it until 30 days before it came due).

> When failure isn't an option, nothing serves a person better than strategic thinking.

When failure isn't an option, nothing serves better than strategic thinking. Evelyn Ryan would have been content to write an occasional poem and submit it to her local paper. But she needed to do something to help her family survive. "A husband and father like my dad was never going to change," her daughter observed. "The only hope for our family depended on the way *she* could change and raise happy and healthy kids to boot."[41] And Evelyn succeeded. Not only did she keep her family afloat; she helped them to become successful. Seven of her children graduated from college, one earned a Ph.D. and another a law degree.

PLAN YOUR LIFE, LIVE YOUR PLAN

While I've never had to face the difficult circumstances Evelyn Ryan did, I have unleashed the power of strategic thinking. For example, I am very strategic in the area of time management. I've observed that most people try to plan their lives one day at a time. They wake up, make up their to-do list, and dive into action (although some people aren't even *that* strategic).

Fewer individuals plan their lives one week at a time. They review their calendar for the week, check their appointments, review their goals, and then get to work. They generally out-achieve most of their daily-planning colleagues. I try to take planning one step further.

At the beginning of every month, I spend half a day working on my calendar for the next forty days. Forty days works for me rather than just thirty. That way, I get a jump on the next month and don't get surprised. (I also do an annual planning session, but I'll tell you more about that in the reflective thinking section.) I begin by reviewing my travel schedule and planning activities with my family. Then I review what projects, lessons, and other objectives I want to accomplish during those five to six weeks. Then I start blocking out days and times for thinking, writing, working, meeting with people, etc. I set times to do fun things, such as seeing a show, watching a ball game, or playing golf. I also set aside small blocks of time to compensate for the unexpected. By the time I'm done, I can tell you nearly everything I'll be doing, almost hour by hour, during the coming weeks. This strategy is one of the reasons I have been able to accomplish much.

WHY YOU SHOULD RELEASE THE
POWER OF STRATEGIC THINKING

Strategic thinking helps me to plan, to become more efficient, to maximize my strengths, and to find the most direct path toward achieving any objective. The benefits of strategic thinking are numerous. Here are a few of the reasons you should adopt it as one of your thinking tools:

1. Strategic Thinking Simplifies the Difficult

Strategic thinking is really nothing more than planning on steroids. Spanish novelist Miguel de Cervantes said, "The man who is prepared has his battle half fought." Strategic thinking takes complex issues and long-term objectives, which can be very difficult to address, and breaks them down into manageable sizes. Anything becomes simpler when it has a plan!

Strategic thinking can also help you simplify the management of everyday life. I do that by using systems, which are nothing more than good strategies repeated. I am well known among pastors and other speakers for my filing system. Writing a lesson or speech can be difficult. But because I use my system to file quotes, stories, and articles, when I need something to flesh out or illustrate a point, I simply go to one of my 1,200 files and find a good piece of material that works.

> "The man who is prepared has his battle half fought."
> —Miguel de Cervantes

I use systems for everything. I have a system for getting in and out of airports quickly and efficiently. I listen to at least seven instructional tapes in the car every week. When I go to meetings, I take people with me who will need to carry the ball afterward so that I rarely have to repeat information or instructions. I take projects with me on airplanes and books into waiting rooms. My wife and I even have a system for how we shop so that if we get separated or have to meet each other, we can find each other in five minutes—even in an area several blocks long—without having to stand around and wait. Just about any difficult task can be made simpler with strategic thinking.

2. Strategic Thinking Prompts You to Ask the Right Questions

Do you want to break down complex or difficult issues? Then ask questions. Strategic thinking forces you through this process. Take a look at the following questions developed by my friend Bobb Biehl, the author of *Masterplanning*.

- *Direction:* What should we do next? Why?

- *Organization:* Who is responsible for what? Who is responsible for whom? Do we have the right people in the right places?

- *Cash:* What is our projected income, expense, net? Can we afford it? How can we afford it?

- *Tracking:* Are we on target?

- *Overall Evaluation:* Are we achieving the quality we expect and demand of ourselves?

- *Refinement:* How can we be more effective and more efficient (move toward the ideal)?[42]

These may not be the only questions you need to ask to begin formulating a strategic plan, but they are certainly a good start.

3. Strategic Thinking Prompts Customization

General George S. Patton observed, "Successful generals make plans to fit circumstances, but do not try to create circumstances to fit plans." On December 19, 1945, Patton, commanding general Dwight D. Eisenhower, and generals Bradley and Devers met in Verdun to discuss how to combat the last great German counteroffensive of World War II, known to history as the Battle of the Bulge. The trapped 101st Airborne Division needed to be rescued, and quickly.

It was decided that Patton should attack the southern flank of the Bulge with his Third Army. Patton had three divisions at his disposal and had calculated that he would be ready to stage his offensive in four days. Eisenhower had a different point of view. Patton recalled,

> General Eisenhower stated that I should wait until I got at least six divisions. I told him that, in my opinion, a prompt attack with three was better than waiting for six—particularly when I did not know where I could get the other three.[43]

Eisenhower agreed to allow Patton to attack, which he did one day ahead of schedule. General Bradley called Patton's actions in the engagement "one of the most astonishing feats of generalship of our campaign in the west."[44] As a result, the Allies contained the German forces, defeated their counteroffensive, and brought the war to an end earlier than it would have otherwise.

All good strategic thinkers are precise in their thinking. They try to match the strategy to the problem, because strategy isn't a one-size-fits-all proposition. Sloppy or generalized thinking is an enemy of achievement. The intention to customize in strategic thinking forces a person to go beyond vague ideas and engage in specific ways to go after a task or problem. It sharpens the mind.

4. Strategic Thinking Prepares You Today for an Uncertain Tomorrow

Peter Drucker, the father of modern management, explains the importance of strategic thinking. He says,

> Strategic planning is necessary precisely because we cannot forecast . . . Strategic planning does not deal with future decisions. It deals with the futurity of present decisions. Decisions exist only in the present. The question that faces the strategic decision-maker is not what his organization should do tomorrow. It is: "What do we have to do today to be ready for uncertain tomorrow?"

Strategic thinking is the bridge that links where you are to where you want to be. It gives direction and credibility today and increases your potential for success tomorrow. It is, as Mary

> Strategic thinking is the bridge that links where you are to where you want to be.

Webb suggests, like saddling your dreams before you ride them.

5. Strategic Thinking Reduces the Margin of Error

Any time you shoot from the hip or go into a totally reactive mode, you increase your margin for error. It's like a golfer stepping up to a golf ball and hitting it before lining up the shot. Misaligning a shot by just a few degrees can send the ball a hundred yards off target. Strategic thinking, however, greatly reduces that margin for error. It lines up your actions with your objectives, just as lining up a shot in golf helps you to put the ball closer to the pin. The better aligned you are with your target, the better the odds that you will be going in the right direction.

6. Strategic Thinking Gives You Influence with Others

One executive confided in another: "Our company has a short range plan and a long range plan. Our short range plan is to stay afloat long enough to make it to our long range plan." That's hardly a strategy, yet that's the position where some business leaders put themselves. There's more than one problem with neglecting strategic thinking in that way. Not only does it fail to build the business, but it also loses the respect of everyone involved with the business.

The one with the plan is the one with the power.

The one with the plan is the one with the power. It doesn't matter in what kind of activity you're involved. Employees want to follow the business leader with a good business plan. Volunteers want to join the pastor with a good ministry plan. Children want to be with the adult who has the well-thought-out vacation plan. If you practice strategic thinking, others will listen to you and they will want to follow you. If you possess a position of leadership in an organization, strategic thinking is essential.

HOW TO RELEASE THE POWER OF STRATEGIC THINKING

To become a better strategic thinker able to formulate and implement plans that will achieve the desired objective, take the following guidelines to heart:

1. Break Down the Issue

My friend Robert Schuller, founder of the Crystal Cathedral, says, "Yard by yard, life is hard; but inch

> "Yard by yard, life is hard; but inch by inch, it's a cinch."
>
> —Robert Schuller

by inch, it's a cinch." The first step in strategic thinking is to break down an issue into smaller, more manageable parts so that you can focus on them more effectively. How you do it is not as important as just doing it. You might break an issue down by function. That's what automotive innovator Henry Ford did when he created the assembly line, and that's why he said, "Nothing is particularly hard if you divide it into small jobs."

You can also break things down according to time. ISS President Dave Sutherland says he likes to compartmentalize topics according to the calendar.

- *Weekdays:* He thinks about daily issues, prioritizing and dealing with the issues of the day.

- *Weekends:* He reserves time to think about topics and issues that will affect the coming 90 to 180 days. He calls it "one step ahead" thinking.

- *Vacations or Scheduled Time Blocks:* He uses to develop long range plans and strategic initiatives that will settle long range issues. He calls that "corporate dreaming" because he finds it fun and refreshing to consider where he's taking the company.

How you break down an issue is up to you, whether it's by function, timetable, responsibility, purpose, or some other method. The point is that you need to break it down. Only one person in a million can juggle the whole thing in his head and think strategically to create solid, viable plans.

2. Ask Why Before How

When most people begin using strategic thinking to solve a problem or plan a way to meet an objective, they often make the mistake of jumping the gun and trying immediately to figure out *how* to accomplish it. Instead of asking *how,* they should first ask *why*. If you jump right into problem solving mode, how are you going to know all the issues?

I fell into this trap in my first job. When I became a senior pastor, I spent the majority of my time working in two areas: counseling and administration. (I graduated from college with a minor in counseling.) So I immediately started to figure out how I could manage those activities. But do you know in what two areas I have absolutely no talent or desire? Counseling and administration! I spent 80 percent of my time in areas of weakness because I never stopped to ask *why*. Solid strategic thinkers always know that unless people are working to correct or bolster an area that needs discipline, they should always spend most of their time working in and developing their areas of strength.

Eugene G. Grace says, "Thousands of engineers can design bridges, calculate strains and stresses, and draw up specifications for machines, but the great engineer is the man who can tell whether the bridge or the machine should be built at all, where it should be built, and when." Asking *why* helps you to think about all the reasons for decisions. It helps you to open your mind to possibilities and opportunities. The size of an opportunity often determines the level of resources and effort that you must invest. Big opportunities allow for big decisions. If you jump to *how* too quickly, you might miss that.

3. Identify the Real Issues and Objectives

William Feather, author of *The Business of Life*, said, "Before it can be solved, a problem must be clearly defined." That's so true. The

> "Before it can be solved, a problem must be clearly defined."
> —William Feather

problem is always to identify the problem. I think too many people rush to solutions, and as a result they end up solving the wrong problem. How do you avoid that? By asking probing questions in an effort to expose the real issues. By challenging all of your assumptions. By collecting information even after you think you've identified the issue. (You may still have to act with incomplete data, but you don't want to jump to a conclusion before you gather enough information to begin identifying the real issue.) Begin by asking, *what else could be the real issue?*

You should also remove any personal agenda. More than almost anything else, that can cloud your judgment. Former GE chairman Jack Welch says,

Strategy is first trying to understand where you sit in today's world. Not where you wish you were or where you hoped you would be, but where you are. Then it's trying to understand where you want to be five years out. Finally, it's assessing the realistic chances of getting from here to there.

Discovering your real situation and objectives is a major part of the battle. Once the real issues are identified, the solutions are often simple.

4. Review Your Resources

> A strategy that doesn't take into account resources is doomed to failure.

I already mentioned how important it is to be aware of your resources, but it bears repeating. A strategy that doesn't take into account resources is doomed to failure. Take an inventory. How much time do you have? How much money? What kinds of materials, supplies, or inventory do you have? What are your other assets? What liabilities or obligations will come into play? Which people on the team can make an impact? You know your own organization and profession. Figure out what resources you have at your disposal.

5. Develop Your Plan

How you approach the planning process depends greatly on your profession and the size of the challenge that you're planning to tackle, so it's difficult to recommend many specifics. However, Rolf Smith, the author of *The 7 Levels of Change: The Guide to Innovation in the World's Largest Corporations*, does have some good advice that I think can help you. As the title of his book suggests, he outlines seven kinds of change, which may prompt you in your planning process:

Level 1: Effectiveness—Doing the right things
Level 2: Efficiency—Doing the right things right
Level 3: Improving—Doing things better
Level 4: Cutting—Doing away with things
Level 5: Adapting—Doing things other people are doing
Level 6: Different—Doing things no one else is doing
Level 7: Impossible—Doing things that can't be done

No matter how you go about planning, take this advice: Start with the obvious. When you tackle an issue or plan that way, it brings unity and consensus to the team, because everyone sees those things. Obvious elements build mental momentum and initiate creativity and intensity. The best way to create a road to the complex is to build on the fundamentals.

6. *Put the Right People in the Right Place*

It's critical that you include your team as part of your strategic thinking. Before you can implement your plan, you must make sure that you have the right people in place. Even the best strategic thinking won't help if you don't take into account the people part of the equation. Look at what happens if you miscalculate:

Wrong Person: Problems instead of Potential
Wrong Place: Frustration instead of Fulfillment
Wrong Plan: Grief instead of Growth

Everything comes together, however, when you put together all three elements: the right person, the right place, and the right plan.

7. *Keep Repeating the Process*

My friend Olan Hendrix remarked, "Strategic thinking is like showering, you have to keep doing it." If you expect to solve any major

> "Strategic thinking is like showering, you have to keep doing it."
> —Olan Hendrix

problem once, you're in for disappointment. Little things—such as filing or shopping systematically—can be won easily

151

> "The will to win is worthless if you do not have the will to prepare."
>
> —Thane Yost

through systems and personal discipline. But major issues need major strategic thinking time. What Thane Yost said is really true: "The will to win is worthless if you do not have the will to prepare." If you want to be an effective strategic thinker, then you need to become a continuous strategic thinker.

As I was working on this chapter, I came across an article in my local paper on the celebration of the Jewish Passover and how millions of American Jews read the order of service for their Seder, or Passover meal, from a small booklet produced by Maxwell House Coffee. For more than seventy years, the coffee company has produced the booklet, called a *Haggada*, and during those years it has distributed more than 40 million copies of it.

"I remember using them all my life," said Regina Witt, who is in her fifties. So does her mother, who is almost ninety. "It's our tradition. I think it would be very strange not to use them."[45]

So how did Maxwell House come to supply the booklets? It was the result of strategic thinking. Eighty years ago, marketing man Joseph Jacobs advised that the company could sell coffee during Passover if the product were certified kosher by a rabbi. (Since 1923, Maxwell House coffee has been certified Kosher for Passover.) And then Jacobs suggested that if they gave away the Haggada booklets, they could increase sales.[46] They've been creating the booklets—and selling coffee during Passover—ever since. That's what can happen when you unleash the power of strategic thinking.

THINKING QUESTION

Am I implementing strategic plans that give me direction for today and increase my potential for tomorrow?

Putting Strategic Thinking into Action

1. Might you be missing opportunities because you have been too quick to ask *how* instead of *why*? Think about a major objective for which you are currently planning. Set aside one hour a day for a week to ask nothing but *why* questions concerning your objective. You can invite people to brainstorm with you at some point, but spend the majority of the time just thinking alone. Be particularly alert for any opportunities that you had not yet seen.

2. What are you currently doing that is not strategic for you? You may be spending more hours than you should working in areas of weakness, just as I did on my first job. Take some time to create an inventory of your personal strengths and then match it against your calendar and to-do list (or a log tracking your activities over a month). If your talents and resources don't match up with your activities, then you need to dedicate some strategic thinking time to figure out how you can make a transition.

Strengths   % of Time

_____   _____

_____   _____

_____   _____

_____   _____

_____   _____

3. If you have a track record of misdiagnosing problems and applying the wrong kinds of solutions to them, you need to spend some time with a good strategic thinker. Find people whose wisdom and discernment you admire, who have a history of successful problem solving, and spend some time with them. Ask to sit in on problem-solving meetings as an observer. Take problems to them for brainstorming sessions. The idea is to learn how they think so that you can begin to develop similar thinking strategies. Whom would you most like to meet with?

_____

_____

4. Create a thinking schedule similar to the one Dave Sutherland uses. Dedicate specific blocks of time to specific issues. Don't forget to break them down so that you can really focus.

Skill 6

Feel the Energy of Possibility Thinking

> *"Nothing is so embarrassing as watching someone do something that you said could not be done."*
> —SAM EWING

What Were They Thinking?

> *"They're multipurpose. Not only do they put the clips on, but they take them off."*
> —CONTRACTOR'S EXPLANATION OF $1,000 PLIERS SOLD TO THE AIR FORCE

In 1975, filmmaker George Lucas went to see Doug Trumbull, the man with the best reputation for special effects in Hollywood. Trumbull was the expert who had worked on *2001: A Space Odyssey*, the first film that gave space travel a realistic feel and look. Lucas was young and relatively inexperienced. He had made only two feature films for theatrical release, but he had proven himself in the business by writing and directing *American Graffiti*, which received critical acclaim and achieved huge financial returns.

Lucas had a vision for the new film he wanted to make. It was to be a story in a science fiction setting that would be part swashbuckling adventure, part Arthurian quest, and part western-style showdown—all rolled into one. In his own words, Lucas said, "It's science fiction—Flash Gordon genre; *2001* meets James Bond, outer space and space ships flying in it."[47] Lucas spoke to Trumbull because he wanted to create scenes with fast-moving ships zooming through space, similar to the way airplanes are filmed in a dogfight. It had never been done. Up to that point, space movies looked like either the technically unsophisticated original *Star Trek* television series or the slow-moving but realistic *2001*.

Author and filmmaker Thomas G. Smith, who has led special effects units in Hollywood, says, "The experienced vision effects people didn't take George seriously. They told him such rapid movement would cause a strobing effect on screen."[48] In other words, they told the young Lucus that it was technically impossible, and it couldn't be done. Then they sent Lucas on his way.

BELIEVING IS SEEING

Lucas was not about to give up, even after being turned down by an "expert" in the field. In his mind's eye, he could *see* what he wanted. He believed it could be done—even though it had never been attempted. John Dykstra, a young filmmaker who had worked with Trumbull, believed in Lucas' vision, too. He didn't know how it could be done, either, but he wanted to pursue the possibility. Lucas hired him and created his own special effects company in order to create the images he wanted. He called it Industrial Light and Magic.

Dykstra, who had some experience using computers while filming, started gathering a team of technicians. Together, they designed and built a studio and began inventing and assembling the technology needed to make the impossible possible. Through good thinking and using trial and error, they worked for almost two years to create what Lucas wanted. The result was the movie *Star Wars*. At the time, it was the most technically innovative movie ever made. It was also the most profitable.

Star Wars was a personal vision for Lucas. When he completed it in 1977, he never thought it would be highly successful. He was hoping only to make enough money to bankroll the sequel. He says,

> I thought it was too wacky for the general public. . . . I just said, "Well, I've had my big hit [with *American Graffiti*], and I'm happy. And I'm going to do this kind of crazy thing, and it'll be fun, and that will be that."[49]

When the movie made money—piles of money—he realized that he could complete the other *Star Wars* movies he had envisioned. And Industrial Light and Magic (ILM), the company he founded only to make the special effects for *Star Wars*, would be necessary to help him create these other movies. But ILM quickly grew into something more. It became the company that made other filmmakers' visions come to life—it made the possibilities in their minds possible. Scott Ross, ILM vice president and general manager, says, "We tell directors and writers not to write their scripts based on what their understanding of technology is, [rather] to really roam free and take advantage of their creative spirit."[50]

Industrial Light and Magic has set the standard for special effects for more than two and a half decades. It has provided special effects for eight of the ten highest-grossing movies of all time, and in the process it has won twelve Academy Awards.

But first and foremost, it is George Lucas' tool to help him realize his vision. The technology keeps advancing, and the effects keep getting more sophisticated, yet the company's capabilities never surpass the possibilities Lucas sees in his mind. Lucas reveals,

> You look at the Jabba the Hutt scene in *Return of the Jedi* [the third movie in the series] and say, "Oh, that's what he wanted the cantina in *Star Wars* to be," Or you look at the end battle, and you say, "Oh, that's what the end battle was supposed to be in the first one." But we couldn't have done this movie then. I mean, it just was not humanly possible or even financially possible. So a lot of these things I have finally worked out. I finally got the end battle the way I wanted it.[51]

In the late 1990s, as Lucas began working on the second trilogy of *Star Wars* movies, he again wanted to do the impossible. "When we started [*Episode I: The Phantom Menace*], we said, 'Okay, now we're gonna do it the way we always wanted to do it. We've got the money, we've got the knowledge—this is it.' "[52] The trick, Lucas said, was "learning the difference between the impossible and the merely never-before-done-or-imagined."[53] For Lucas, most things are merely never-before-done-or-imagined, because to him, anything is possible. That's how it is for a practitioner of possibility thinking.

Why You Should Feel the Energy of Possibility Thinking

People who embrace possibility thinking are capable of accomplishing tasks that seem impossible because they believe in solutions. Here are several reasons why you should become a possibility thinker:

1. Possibility Thinking Increases Your Possibilities

When you believe you can do something difficult—and you succeed—many doors open for you. When George Lucas succeeded in making *Star Wars*, many other possibilities opened up to him. Industrial Light and Magic became a source of revenue to help underwrite his own projects. He was able to produce merchandising tie-ins to his movies, thus bringing in another revenue stream to fund his movie making. But his confidence in doing the difficult has also made a huge impact on other movie makers and a whole new generation of movie goers. Popular culture writer Chris Salewicz asserts, "At first directly through

> If you open yourself up to possibility thinking, you open yourself up to many other possibilities.

his own work and then via the unparalleled influence of ILM {Industrial Light and Magic}, George Lucas has dictated for two decades the essential broad notion of what is cinema."[54] If you open yourself up to possibility thinking, you open yourself up to many other possibilities.

2. Possibility Thinking Draws Opportunities and People to You

The case of George Lucas helps you to see how being a possibility thinker can create new opportunities and attract people. If Lucas had not believed *Star Wars* was possible and made the film, few of his other movies would have been made. For that matter, most of the influential and profitable movies of the last twenty years would not have been possible. In the process, some of the most talented people in the world came to work for him at Industrial Light and Magic. In fact, in an industry where creative people usually remain independent, work as freelancers, complete jobs, and then move on, Lucas has managed to assemble a staff that chooses to stay with him.

People who think big attract big people to them. If you want to achieve big things, you need to become a possibility thinker.

3. Possibility Thinking Increases Others' Possibilities

Big thinkers who make things happen also create possibilities for others. That happens, in part, because it's contagious. You can't help but become more confident and think bigger when you're around possibility thinkers. But possibility thinking also impacts others in more direct ways.

Look at what happened in Atlanta, Georgia, in 1987. A real estate attorney named Billy Payne thought it would be possible to bring the Olympics to Atlanta. People told him it couldn't be done. Payne says that at first "the idea was viewed as somewhat eclectic, outrageous, impossible, 'good idea but you'll never win.' "[55] But Payne was undeterred. He kept believing, and working at it. And of course, in 1996, the summer Olympics were held in Atlanta, making a huge impact on the city and its people. The impact continues. Once the city hosted an international event of the magnitude of the Olympics, the people of Atlanta realized that other possibilities were endless.

4. Possibility Thinking Allows You to Dream Big Dreams

> "Big thinkers are specialists in creating positive forward-looking, optimistic pictures in their own minds and in the minds of others."
> —David J. Schwartz

No matter what your profession, possibility thinking can help you to broaden your horizons and dream bigger dreams. Professor David J. Schwartz believes, "Big thinkers are specialists in creating positive forward-looking, optimistic pictures in their own minds and in the minds of others."

In 1970, when I was twenty-three years old, I read a book that made a major impact on how I dream. It was called *Move Ahead with Possibility Thinking* by Robert Schuller. As a young pastor in my first church, it thrilled me to read about how Schuller overcame seemingly impossible circumstances to build a huge church in Garden Grove, California. When I read the following words, my world changed: "The greatest churches have yet to be organized."

Even as a child, I was a positive person. After all, I had grown up in the household of a father who had taught himself to be a positive thinker. But Schuller's book still had a huge impact on my life. The day I read those words, what had been my wildest dreams looked tame. If you embrace possibility thinking, your dreams will go from molehill to mountain size, and because you believe in possibilities, you put yourself in position to achieve them.

5. *Possibility Thinking Makes it Possible to Rise Above Average*

During the 1970s, when oil prices went through the roof, automobile makers were ordered to make their cars more fuel efficient. One manufacturer asked a group of senior engineers to drastically reduce the weight of cars they were designing. They worked on the problem and searched for solutions, but they finally concluded that making lighter cars couldn't be done, would be too expensive, and would present too many safety concerns. They couldn't get out of the rut of their average thinking.

What was the auto maker's solution? They gave the problem to a group of less experienced engineers. The new group found ways to reduce the weight of the company's automobiles by hundreds of pounds. Because they thought that solving the problem was possible, it was. Every time you remove the label of impossible from a task, you raise your potential from average to off the charts.

6. Possibility Thinking Gives You Energy

Thomas Fuller, chaplain to King Charles II of England, observed, "The real difference between men is energy. A strong will, a settled purpose, and invincible determination, can accomplish almost anything; and in this lies the distinction between great men and little men."

A direct correlation exists between possibility thinking and the level of a person's energy. Who gets energized by the prospect of losing? If you know something can't succeed, how much time and energy are you willing to give it? Nobody goes looking for a lost cause.

> You invest yourself in what you believe can succeed.

You invest yourself in what you believe can succeed. When you embrace possibility thinking, you believe in what you're doing, and that gives you energy.

7. Possibility Thinking Keeps You from Giving Up

Above all, possibility thinkers believe they can succeed. Denis Waitley, author of *The Psychology of Winning*, says, "The winners in life think constantly in terms of 'I can, I will and I am.' Losers, on the other hand, concentrate their waking thoughts on what they should have done, or what they don't do." If you believe you can do something, you have already won much of the battle. If you believe you can't, then it doesn't matter how hard you try, because you've already lost.

One of the people who showed himself to be a great possibility thinker in 2001 was New York mayor Rudy Giuliani. In the hours following the World Trade Center tragedy, Giuliani not only led the city through the chaos of the disaster, but he instilled confidence in everyone he touched. Afterward, he gave some insight and perspective on his experience:

> I was so proud of the people I saw on the street. No chaos, but they were frightened and confused, and it seemed to me that they needed to hear from my heart where I thought we were going. I was trying to think, *Where can I go for some comparison to this, some lessons about how to handle it?* So I started thinking about Churchill, started thinking that we're going to have to rebuild the spirit of the city, and what better example than Churchill and the people of London during the Blitz in 1940, who had to keep up their spirit during this sustained bombing? It was a comforting thought.[56]

Sixteen hours after the planes struck the buildings in New York City, when Giuliani finally returned at 2:30 A.M. to his apartment for a rest, instead of sleeping, he read the World War II chapters of a new biography of Winston Churchill. He read how Churchill helped his people to see the possibilities and keep his people going. Inspired, Giuliani did the same for his own people six decades later.

HOW TO FEEL THE ENERGY OF POSSIBILITY THINKING

If you are a naturally positive person who already embraces possibility thinking, then you're already tracking with me. However, some people, rather than being optimistic, are naturally negative or cynical. They believe that possibility thinkers are naive or foolish. If your thinking runs toward pessimism, let me ask you a question: how many highly successful people do you know who are continually negative? How many impossibility thinkers are you acquainted with who achieve big things? None!

People with an it-can't-be-done mindset have two choices. They can expect the worst and continually experience it; or they can change their thinking. That's what George Lucas did. Believe it or not, even though he is a possibility thinker, he is not a naturally positive person. He says, "I'm very cynical, and as a result, I think the defense I have against it is to be optimistic."[57] In other words, he chooses to think positively. He sums it up this way: "As corny as it sounds, the power of positive thinking goes a long way. So determination and positive thinking combined with talent combined with knowing your craft . . . that may sound like a naive point of view, but at the same time it's worked for me and it's worked for all my friends—so I have come to believe it."[58]

If you want possibility thinking to work for you, then begin by following these suggestions:

1. Stop Focusing on the Impossibilities

The first step in becoming a possibility thinker is to stop yourself from searching for and dwelling on what's wrong with any given situation. Sports psychologist Bob Rotella recounts, "I tell people: If you

> "I tell people: If you don't want to get into positive thinking, that's OK. Just eliminate all the negative thoughts from your mind, and whatever's left will be fine."
> —Bob Rotella

don't want to get into positive thinking, that's OK. Just eliminate all the negative thoughts from your mind, and whatever's left will be fine."

If possibility thinking is new to you, you're going to have to give yourself a lot of coaching to eliminate some of the negative self-talk you may hear in your head. When you automatically start listing all the things that can go wrong or all the reasons something can't be done, stop yourself and say, "Don't go there." Then ask, "What's right about this?" That will help to get you started. And if negativity is a really big problem for you and pessimistic things come out of your mouth before you've even thought them through, you may need to enlist the aid of a friend or family member to alert you every time you utter negative ideas.

2. Stay Away from the "Experts"

So-called experts do more to shoot down people's dreams than just about anybody else. In the book *Future Edge*, Joel Barker recounts a few statements made by experts that seem comical now. Those remarks highlight that expertise doesn't prevent someone from selling short a dream. Ponder the following comments, along with when they were made:

- "The phonograph is of no commercial value." —Thomas Edison, remarking on his own invention in 1880.
- "There is no likelihood man can ever tap the power of the atom." —Robert Millikan, Nobel Prize winner in physics, 1920.
- "It is an idle dream to imagine that automobiles will take the place of railways in the long-distance movement of passengers." —American Road Congress, 1913.
- "I think there is a world market for about five computers." —Thomas Watson, chairman IBM, 1943.

- "There is no reason for any individual to have a computer in their home." —Ken Olsen, president of Digital Equipment Corporation, 1977.[59]

And don't forget, the special effects experts told Lucas that the images he wanted to create couldn't be done.

Possibility thinkers are very reluctant to dismiss anything as impossible. Rocket pioneer Wernher von Braun said, "I have learned to use the word impos-

> "The word impossible is not in my dictionary."
> —Napoleon Bonaparte

sible with the greatest of caution." And Napoleon Bonaparte declared, "The word impossible is not in my dictionary." If you feel you must take the advice of an expert, however, then heed the words of John Andrew Holmes, who asserted, "Never tell a young person that something cannot be done. God may have been waiting centuries for somebody ignorant enough of the impossible to do that thing." If you want to achieve something, give yourself permission to believe it is possible—no matter what experts might say.

3. Look for Possibilities in Every Situation

Becoming a possibility thinker is more than just refusing to let yourself be negative. It's something more. It's looking for positive possibilities despite the circumstances. Every situation can be seen as potentially better than it is at present. Possibility thinking is possible even in negative situations.

I recently heard Don Soderquist, former president of Wal-Mart, tell a wonderful story that illustrates how a person can find positive possibilities in any situation. Soderquist had gone with Sam Walton to Huntsville, Alabama, to open several new stores. While there, Walton suggested they visit the competition. Here's what Soderquist said happened:

> We went into one [store], and I have to tell you that it was the worst store I've ever seen in my life. It was terrible. There were no customers. There was no help on the floor. The aisles were cluttered with merchandise, empty shelves, dirty, it was absolutely terrible. He [Walton] walked one way and I'd walk the other way and we'd kind of meet out on the side walk. He said, "What'd you think, Don?"
>
> I said, "Sam, that is the absolutely worst store I've ever seen in my life. I mean, did you see the aisles?"
>
> He said, "Don, did you see the pantyhose rack?"
>
> I said, "No, I didn't, Sam. I must have gone on a different aisle than you. I didn't see that."
>
> He said, "That was the best pantyhose rack I've ever seen, Don." And he said, "I pulled the fixture out and on the back was the name of the manufacturer. When we get back, I want you to call that manufacturer and have him come in and visit with our fixture people. I want to put that rack in our stores. It's absolutely the best I've ever seen." And he said next, "Did you see the ethnic cosmetics?"
>
> I said, "Sam, that must have been right next to the panty hose rack, because I absolutely missed that."
>
> He said, "Don, do you realize that in our stores we have four feet of ethnic cosmetics. These people had 12 feet of it. We are absolutely missing the boat. I wrote down the distributor of some of those products. When we get back, I want you to get a hold of our cosmetic buyer and get these people in. We absolutely need to expand our ethnic cosmetics."

Now, Sam Walton didn't hit me on the head and say,

"Don, now what lesson did you learn from this?" He had already hit me on the head by looking for the good, looking how to improve, striving for excellence. It's so easy to go and look at what other people do badly. But one of the leadership characteristics of vision that he showed me, and I'll never forget it, is look for the good in what other people are doing and apply it.[60]

It doesn't take a genius IQ or twenty years of experience to find the possibility in every situation. All it takes is the right attitude, and anybody can cultivate that.

4. Dream One Size Bigger

One of the best ways to cultivate a possibility mind-set is to prompt yourself to dream one size bigger than you normally do. Let's face it: most people dream too small. They don't think big enough. Henry Curtis advises, "Make your plans as fantastic as you like, because twenty-five years from now, they will seem mediocre. Make your plans ten times as great as you first planned, and twenty-five years from now you will wonder why you did not make them fifty times as great."

> One of the best ways to cultivate a possibility mind-set is to prompt yourself to dream one size bigger than you normally do.

People need BHAGs—big hairy audacious goals—as the authors of *Built to Last* maintain. If you push yourself to dream more expansively, to imagine your organization one size bigger, to make your goals at least a step beyond what makes you comfortable, you will be forced to grow. And it will set you up to believe in greater possibilities.

5. *Question the Status Quo*

Most people want their lives to keep improving, yet they value peace and stability at the same time. People often forget that you can't improve and still stay the same. Growth means change. Change requires challenging the status quo. If you want greater possibilities, you can't settle for what you have now.

When you become a possibility thinker, you will face many people who will want you to give up your dreams and embrace the status quo. As you meet them, take the advice of the poet who penned the following words:

> Beware of those who stand aloof
> And greet each venture with reproof;
> The world would stop if things were run
> By men who say, "It can't be done."[61]

Achievers refuse to accept the status quo. As you begin to explore greater possibilities for yourself, your organization, or your family—and others challenge you for it—take comfort in knowing that *right now* as you read this, other possibility thinkers across the country and around the world are thinking about curing cancer, developing new energy sources, feeding hungry people, and improving quality of life. They are challenging the status quo against the odds—and you should, too.

6. *Find Inspiration from Great Achievers*

You can learn a lot about possibility thinking by studying great achievers. I began this chapter telling you about George Lucas. Perhaps he doesn't appeal to you, or you don't like the movie industry. (Personally, I'm not a big science fiction fan, but I admire Lucas as a thinker, creative visionary, and businessperson.) Find some achievers you admire and study them. Look for people with the attitude of Robert F. Kennedy, who popularized George Bernard Shaw's stirring statement: "Some men see things as they are and say, 'Why?' I dream of things that never were and say, 'Why not?'"

I know possibility thinking isn't in style with many people. So call it what you like: the will to succeed, belief in yourself, confidence in your ability, faith. It's really true: people who believe they can't, don't. But if you believe you can, you can! That's the power of possibility thinking.

THINKING QUESTION

Am I unleashing the enthusiasm of possibility thinking to find solutions for even seemingly impossible situations?

Putting Possibility Thinking into Action

1. Everyone has dreams. And many times those dreams get shot down by others. If you are not in the habit of big thinking—if you've had your possibility thinking put down in the past— then you need to try to recapture those dreams.

Think back to a time when you were more likely to imagine yourself doing great things. (You may need to go all the way back to your childhood.) What did you dream about? What was the thing in your heart that you *really* wanted to do? Recapture that thought, explore it, and do some dreaming with it.

_____

_____

_____

2. The dream you had earlier in life may not be possible for you now. (Although many are, if you're willing and able to pay the price.) So, what do you really want to do? What is your dream? If you didn't fear failure or being laughed at, what would you do today? Write that down. Then think about what would be necessary to accomplish it. The best way to do that is to look down the road ten years and 90 days. Looking ahead ten years will help you set the direction in terms of the big picture. Looking ahead 90 days will help identify specific steps to get the process started.

_____

_____

_____

3. This week, read a biography of someone you admire. If you have the time and energy, read two or three about the same person. Make notes concerning how that person harnessed the energy of possibility thinking. Then find three to five principles or practices from that person's life that you can apply to your own. Write them here:

_____

_____

_____

_____

_____

Skill 7

Embrace the Lessons of Reflective Thinking

"To doubt everything or to believe everything are two equally convenient solutions; both dispense with the necessity of reflection."
—JULES HENRI POINCARÉ

What Were They Thinking?

"Ever since I was a kid, I've always been a real deep thinker and stuff."
—BILLY RAY CYRUS, country music singer

As I work on this chapter, I sit at my desk in my home office, surrounded by items that help me to reflect on an almost continual basis and to get my work done quickly and efficiently.

On the left side of my desk, I have folders for the projects on which I am currently working. Each folder is a different color so that I can quickly identify it. Green holds ideas, quotes, and stories for this book. Purple is for personal issues and ideas related to my companies. A blue folder contains thoughts I'm gathering for my next book. Each folder has a list of questions, hand-written on the outside, to prompt my thinking or keep me on track as I collect ideas.

On the far side of my desk, across from me, are pictures of people important to me. There's a picture of my wife, Margaret, taken on a trip to Europe years ago; a picture of my beautiful daughter, Elizabeth, taken when she was a senior in high school; and another of Joel Porter, my son, standing with me next to a monument of John Wesley in England. There are up-to-date pictures of both of our children with their spouses, Elizabeth with Steve and Joel Porter with Elisabeth (yes, it's confusing that our daughter and daughter-in-law have the same names). And of course, there are numerous pictures of Maddie and Hannah, the apples of their grandfather's eyes! As I look at them, I am constantly reminded of what's most important in my life.

On the right side of my desk are file folders containing the main lectures I will be giving this year. I like to keep them close so that I can continually update them and refer to them. The ones for events that I will be leading in the next two weeks are in yellow folders so that I can focus additional attention on them.

And right in front of me are three items within easy reach. The first is the legal pad I'm writing on now. My current project stays front and center—even if I go to an appointment in the morning or quit for the day. I want to be able to dive into the material in a moment. Next to that is my communication pad. If I want to share an experience with Margaret or if I need to remember to tell something to my assistant, Linda, I jot it down there. The third item is a small leather-bound pad that I call my idea pad. I try to capture what I call my thought of the day (I try to produce one good thought each day) or any other ideas on which I want to be able to reflect.

WHAT DO YOU HAVE COOKING?

I like to think of my desk as a stove—it's always got a lot of things cooking on it. Each item has its place, and at any given moment, I might take a "pot" from a back burner, where it has been simmering for days, weeks, or even months, and move it to the front burner so that I can actively work on it or even finish it off.

Reflective thinking is a major part of my life and has been for decades. I'm constantly reflecting and reviewing my life so that I can both keep growing and keep celebrating victories. I got into the habit of thinking reflectively as a pastor. Because churches function on a weekly cycle, I used to spend time every Sunday night reviewing the previous week, reflecting on the effectiveness of the weekend's activities and evaluating everything in order to prepare for the coming week. As I saw the value of that kind of reflection, I began to spend at least a few minutes every day reflecting. Each time I ask myself three questions:

- What did I learn today?
- What should I share?
- What must I do?

I've found that asking myself these questions helps me to stay disciplined and accountable for how I spend my time.

I've already explained how I review my calendar every month and look at the forty days ahead. But I also employ another invaluable calendar exercise in the area of reflective thinking. At the end of each December, I spend time reflecting on the past year. First, I take my calendar for the year and review how I spent my time. I think and process and pray about the year.

Then I capture some thoughts on paper. Here are the kinds of things I thought about concerning the year 2001:

- Highlights with Margaret (31 entries)
- Personal Highlights (23 entries)
- Low Points (11 entries)
- Major Events (9 entries)
- #1 Personal Highlight
- #1 Business Highlight
- International Conferences (4 entries)
- Personal Reflections of Significance (8 entries)

As I go through this process, my goal is to reflect on how I spent a year of my life so that I might learn from my successes and mistakes, discover what I should try to repeat, and determine what I should change. It is always a valuable exercise. By mentally visiting past situations, you can think with greater understanding. Reflective thinking is like the crock-pot of the mind. It encourages your thoughts to simmer until they're done.

> Reflective thinking is like the crock-pot of the mind. It encourages your thoughts to simmer until they're done.

WHY YOU SHOULD EMBRACE THE LESSONS OF REFLECTIVE THINKING

The pace of our society does not encourage reflective thinking. Most people would rather act than think. Now, don't get me wrong. I'm a person of action. I have very high energy and I like to see things accomplished. But I'm also a reflective thinker. I know how valuable it is:

Embrace the Lessons of Reflective Thinking

1. Reflective Thinking Gives You True Perspective

When our children were young and still lived at home, we used to take them on wonderful vacations every year. When we got home, they always knew that I was going to ask them two questions: "What did you like best?" and "What did you learn?" It didn't matter whether we went to Walt Disney World or Washington, D.C.

I always asked those questions. Why? Because I wanted them to reflect on their experiences. Children don't naturally grasp the value (or cost) of an experience unless prompted. They take things for granted. I wanted my children to appreciate our trips and to learn from them. When you reflect, you are able to put an experience into perspective. You are able to evaluate its timing. And you are able to gain a new appreciation for things that before went unnoticed. Most people are able to recognize the sacrifices of their parents or other people only when they become parents themselves. That's the kind of perspective that comes with reflection.

> When you reflect, you are able to put an experience into perspective.

2. Reflective Thinking Gives Emotional Integrity to Your Thought Life

Few people have good perspective in the heat of an emotional moment. Most individuals who enjoy the thrill of an experience try to go back and recapture it without first trying to evaluate it. (It's one of the reasons our culture produces so many thrill seekers.) Likewise, those who survive a traumatic experience usually avoid similar situations at all costs, which sometimes ties them into emotional knots.

Reflective thinking enables you to distance yourself from the

> Reflective thinking enables you to distance yourself from the intense emotions of particularly good or bad experiences and see them with fresh eyes.

intense emotions of particularly good or bad experiences and see them with fresh eyes. You can see the thrills of the past in the light of emotional maturity and examine tragedies in the light of truth and logic. That process can help a person to stop carrying around a bunch of negative emotional baggage.

President George Washington observed, "We ought not to look back unless it is to derive useful lessons from past errors, and for the purpose of profiting by dearly bought experience." Any feeling that can stand up to the light of truth and can be sustained over time has emotional integrity and is therefore worthy of your mind and heart.

3. Reflective Thinking Increases Your Confidence in Decision-making

Have you ever made a snap judgment and later wondered if you did the right thing? Everybody has. Reflective thinking can help to diffuse that doubt. It also gives you confidence for the next decision. Once you've reflected on an issue, you don't have to repeat every step of the thinking process when you're faced with it again. You've got mental road markers from having been there before. That compresses and speeds up thinking time—and it gives you confidence. And over time, it can also strengthen your intuition.

During my early years of leadership, I wasn't strong at reflective thinking. When confronted by a challenge, I often tried to wing it or rely on my intuition. Although those methods frequently served me well personally, I found it hard to teach others how to meet challenges effectively. When another leader asked for advice, my response often led to frustration. No one wants to hear, "Wait until the timing is right, then just trust your instincts."

In order to mentor others more successfully, I began to invest more time in reflective thinking. After I made an important decision, I took the time to ask myself these questions:

- What factors played a role in my decision?
- What steps did I take in making the decision?
- Was my decision a good one? Why or why not?

By going through these steps, I came to understand how both good and bad decisions are made, and I became better able to pass that information on to others. As a result, my confidence increased, and so did that of others.

4. Reflective Thinking Clarifies the Big Picture

When you engage in reflective thinking, you can put ideas and experiences into a more accurate context. Reflective thinking encourages us to go back and spend time pondering what we have done and what we have seen. If a person who loses his job reflects on what happened, he may see a pattern of events that led to his dismissal. He will better understand what happened, why it happened, and what things were his responsibility. If he also looks at the incidents that occurred afterward, he may realize that in the larger scheme of things, he's better off in his new position because it better fits his skills and desires. Without reflection, it can be very difficult to see that big picture.

I benefit in the area of communication from the big-picture results of reflective thinking. Before I speak to a company, for example, I spend time learning as much as I can about the organization. I do it because I want to have the big picture in mind as I prepare to speak to their people. One of the main differences between a good speech and a great one is customization.

After I have finished my presentation, I again spend time in reflective thinking. I often do this on the plane while flying to my next engagement. I reflect on the response of the audience, the comments of the leaders, and the feedback I received from those who extended me the invitation. *Did I apply the principles specifically to the people in the audience? Did I connect with them? Did I give them a plan of action they could follow? Did I meet my expectations, which are set even higher than those of my sponsor? Do I need to follow up in any way?*

By going through this process every time I speak, reflecting both before and after my talk, I see the big picture and use it to my best advantage.

5. Reflective Thinking Takes a Good Experience and Makes it a Valuable Experience

When you were just starting out in your career, did it seem that few people were willing to give someone without experience an opportunity? At the same time, could you see people who had been on their jobs twenty years who yet did their work poorly? If so, that probably frustrated you.

Playwright William Shakespeare wrote, "Experience is a jewel, and it had need be so, for it is often purchased at an infinite rate." Yet, experience alone does not add value to a life. It's not necessarily experience that is valuable; it's the insight people gain because of their experience. Reflective thinking turns experience into insight.

> Reflective thinking turns experience into insight.

Mark Twain said, "We should be careful to get out of an experience all the wisdom that is in it—not like the cat that sits

180

down on a hot stove lid. She will never sit down on a hot stove lid again—and that is well; but also she will never sit down on a cold one anymore."[62] An experience becomes valuable when it informs or equips us to meet new experiences. Reflective thinking helps to do that.

HOW TO EMBRACE THE LESSONS OF REFLECTIVE THINKING

If you are like most people in our culture today, you probably do very little reflective thinking. If that's the case, it may be holding you back more than you think. Take to heart the following suggestions to increase your ability to think reflectively:

1. Set Aside Time for Reflection

Greek philosopher Socrates observed, "The unexamined life is not worth living." For most people, however, reflection and self-examination doesn't come naturally. It can be a fairly uncomfortable activity for a variety of reasons: they have a hard time staying focused; they find the process dull; or they don't like spending a lot of time

> "The unexamined life is not worth living."
> —Socrates

thinking about emotionally difficult issues. But if you don't carve out the time for it, you are unlikely to do any reflective thinking.

2. Remove Yourself from Distractions

As much as any other kind of thinking, reflection requires solitude. Distraction and reflection simply don't mix. It's not the kind of thing you can do well near a television, in a cubicle, while the phone is ringing, or with children in the same room.

One of the reasons I've been able to accomplish much and keep growing personally is that I've not only set aside time to reflect, but I've separated myself from distractions for short blocks of time: thirty minutes in the spa; an hour outside on a rock in my back yard; or a few hours in a comfortable chair in my office. The place doesn't matter—as long as you remove yourself from distractions and interruptions.

3. Regularly Review Your Calendar or Journal

Most people use their calendar as a planning tool, which it is. But few people use it as a reflective thinking tool. What could be better, however, for helping you to review where you have been and what you have done—except maybe a journal? I'm not a journaler in the regular sense; I don't use writing to figure out what I'm thinking and feeling. Instead, I figure out what I'm thinking and feeling, and then I write down significant thoughts and action points. (I file the thoughts so that I can quickly put my hands on them again. I immediately execute the action points or delegate them to someone else.)

Calendars and journals remind you of how you've spent your time, show you whether your activities match your priorities, and help you see whether you are making progress. They also offer you an opportunity to recall activities that you might not have had the time to reflect on previously. Because of my busy schedule, I often have to go from speaking engagement to meeting to speaking engagement without any kind of break, and then have to pack up and travel to another city that night. If something significant happens during that trip and I miss the chance to think about it, a review of my calendar reminds me to give that significant event or meeting some thought time. I try never to allow a major event to pass without having a few moments of reflection afterward. Some of the most valuable thoughts you've ever had may have been lost because you didn't give yourself the reflection time you needed.

4. Ask the Right Questions

The value you receive from reflecting will depend on the kinds of questions you ask yourself. The better the questions, the more gold you will mine from your thinking. When I reflect, I think in terms of my values, relationships, and experiences. Here are some sample questions from each area:

> The value you receive from reflecting will depend on the kinds of questions you ask yourself.

THINKING RELATED TO VALUES

- *Personal Growth:* What have I learned today that will help me grow? How can I apply it to my life? When should I apply it?

- *Adding Value:* To whom did I add value today? How do I know I added value to that person? Can I follow up and compound the positive benefit he or she received?

- *Teamwork:* What did I do with someone else that made both of us better? Would the other person agree that it was a win/win? Can we do something else together to continue our mutual success?

- *Leadership:* Did I lead by example today? Did I lift my people and organization to a higher level? What did I do and how did I do it?

- *Physical Health:* Did I exercise at my optimal heart rate for thirty-five minutes today? Have I exercised at least five times in the last seven days? Did I stay on my low-fat diet today?

- *Personal Faith:* Did I represent God well today? Did I practice the Golden Rule? Have I "walked the second mile" with someone?

THINKING RELATED TO RELATIONSHIPS

- *Marriage and Family:* Did I communicate love to Margaret, the children, and the grandchildren today? How did I show that love? Did they feel it? Did they return it?

- *Friends:* Have I been a good friend this week? To whom? What did I do? Is there something else I need to do? Is there another friend who needs me?

- *Inner Circle:* Have I spent enough time with my key players? What can I do to help them be more successful? In what areas can I mentor them?

- *God:* Have I spent time with God? What is he teaching me now? Am I learning? Am I obeying? Have I continually talked with him today?

THINKING RELATED TO EXPERIENCES

- *Discoveries:* What did I encounter today to which I need to give more thinking time? Are there lessons to be learned? Are there things to be done?

- *Memories:* Did I create a good memory for someone today? Was it because of a comment, an action, or a shared experience?

- *Difficulties:* What went wrong? Could I have changed it? What do I need to do differently next time?

- *Successes:* What went right? Did I create it? Is there a principle I can learn from the experience?

- *People:* Whom did I meet? What were my impressions?

- *Conclusions:* Have I closed my day appropriately? Have I expressed gratitude? Have I learned something, loved someone? Have I enjoyed and lived the day to the fullest?

How you organize your reflection time is up to you. You may want to adapt my pattern to your own values. Or you can try a system that my friend Dick Biggs uses. He creates three columns on a sheet of paper:

Year   Turning Point   Impact

This system is good for reflecting on the bigger picture. Dick used it to see patterns in his life, such as when he moved to Atlanta and was encouraged by a new teacher to write. You could just as easily write "Event," "Significance," and "Action Point" on a page to help you benefit from reflective thinking. The main thing is to create questions that work for you, and write down any significant thoughts that come to you during the reflection time.

5. Cement Your Learning Through Action

Writing down the good thoughts that come out of your reflective thinking has value, but nothing helps you to grow like putting your thoughts into action. To do that, you must be intentional. When you read a good book, for example, there are always good thoughts, quotes, or lessons that you can take away from it and use yourself. I always mark the takeaways in a book and then reread them when I'm done with the book. When I listen to a message, I record the takeaways so that I can file them for future use. When I go to a seminar, I take good notes, and I use a system of symbols to cue me to do certain things:

- An arrow like this → means to look at this material again.
- An asterisk like this * next to a marked section means to file it according to the subject noted.
- A bracket like this [means that I want to use what's marked in a lecture or book.
- An arrow like this ↑ means this idea will take off if I work at it.

When most people go to a conference or seminar, they enjoy the experience, listen to the speakers, and sometimes even take notes. But nothing happens after they go home. They like many of the concepts they hear, but when they close their notebooks, they don't think about them again. When that happens, they receive little more than a temporary surge of motivation. When you go to a conference, revisit what you heard, reflect on it, and then put it into action, it can change your life.

Ultimately, reflective thinking has three main values: it gives me perspective within context; it allows me to continually connect with my journey; and it provides counsel and direction concerning my future. It is an invaluable tool to my personal growth. Few things in life can help me learn and improve the way reflective thinking can.

BORROWING ANOTHER'S WISDOM

The lessons to be learned through reflective thinking don't always have to come from your own experience. In January of 2002 the King family asked me to speak on the leadership of Martin Luther King, Jr., at Ebenezer Baptist Church in downtown Atlanta for Martin Luther King Day. I've always had great admiration for King. He was an incredible leader. I'm not alone; people asked to identify the greatest influence in the world during the twentieth century commonly identify Martin Luther King, Jr.

As I prepared my brief message and reviewed his accomplishments, I noticed how reflective thinking shaped his approach to racism and civil rights issues. As a young man growing up in the South, King had suffered under Jim Crow laws and segregation. His experience birthed a desire to change the situation of African-Americans in the United States. To solve the problems of the present and secure a better future for his people, he reflected on the past to learn its lessons. In college, he read Henry David Thoreau's essay "Civil Disobedience." King felt impressed by Thoreau's assertion that citizens had the right to disobey unjust laws. In fact, Thoreau went to jail rather than pay his taxes, which he believed were being used to support slavery.

THE POWER OF REFLECTION

King undoubtedly continued to reflect on Thoreau's ideas as he wrestled with the problems of segregation and racism. Then in 1948, while studying for the ministry at Crozer Theological Seminary in Pennsylvania, he heard A. J. Muste and Mordecai W. Johnson teach about Mohandas Gandhi, also strongly influenced by Thoreau's writings. After that, King began to study

Gandhi seriously.[63] He found that while Thoreau's philosophy promoted the idea of individual civil disobedience, Gandhi had made it a vehicle of the masses. Gandhi used it to liberate the people of India from British rule. King decided to use similar tactics in the United States.

In the 1950s and '60s, King dominated the civil rights scene. More than anyone else, he made white America wake up to problems of racism and segregation and led black America's fight against the inherently corrupt and oppressive system. The Montgomery Bus Boycott of 1955; the lunch counter sit-ins to desegregate restaurants in the South; the freedom rides in 1961; the fight to desegregate schools; the march from Selma to Montgomery, Alabama; the march on Washington; and many other events during the civil rights movement were strongly influenced by King's leadership. And every one of them displays the influence of his reflective thinking.

Reflective thinking in the hands of Martin Luther King, Jr., radically transformed American life. If you embrace it as King did, you may not be able to change the world, but you can certainly change your life.

THINKING QUESTION

Am I regularly revisiting the past to gain a true perspective and think with understanding?

Putting Reflective Thinking into Action

1. Create a daily reflection time to help you learn from the events of your day and to capture your ideas. Set aside a regular

time and place to do your reflecting. Practice the discipline of daily reflective thinking for twenty-one days.

2. Figure out what questions to ask yourself during your reflective thinking times. Review the sample questions in the chapter. Then create your own set of questions. Begin by creating general questions to be used after any event or meeting. Then create more specific questions related to your values and relationships.

_____

_____

_____

_____

_____

3. At the end of this month, set aside a block of two to four hours to do a review of your calendar from the past month. Review your appointments. Check your to-do lists. Figure out where you spent your time and whether you did so wisely. As you look at individual entries, ask yourself:

- Have I already reflected on this event?
- What went right?
- What went wrong?
- What did I learn?
- What can I do differently next time?

Don't forget to write down insights to be filed and action points to be completed.

4. The next time you go to a conference, schedule an hour-long reflection time for a few days after the conference. Then when you attend the event, take good notes and use some kind of system of symbols to mark your notes as you write. Then when your scheduled reflection time rolls around, review your notes. Once again, for each good idea either file it, share it with someone, or create an action point from it.

Skill 8

Question the Acceptance of Popular Thinking

"I'm not an answering machine, I'm a questioning machine. If we have all the answers, how come we're in such a mess?"
—DOUGLAS CARDINAL

What Were They Thinking?

"Everything that can be invented has been invented."
—CHARLES H. DUELL,
director of the U.S. Patent Office, 1899

Until December 18, 1998, I took my health almost for granted. I was fifty-one years old, had a high energy level and had never experienced any kind of medical problem. But on the night of my organization's Christmas party, I suffered a serious heart attack. My life has changed a lot since then. Now I watch my diet, exercise every day, and am even more intentional in expressing my love to the important people in my life. The heart attack has also made me much more aware of issues related to health. That's how I came to read about Paul

Ridker, a cardiologist who challenged popular thinking and who is changing the way doctors think about patients' risk of heart attacks.

HE'S GOT HEART

Ridker traces his interest in medicine to a rare immune disorder he suffered as a child. He got very sick when he and his family returned to the U.S. from India. Doctors discovered that parasites were attacking his body. Fortunately, they were able to cure him, but the experience immersed him in the world of medicine at a tender age. Eventually it became his passion.

After receiving his undergraduate degree from Brown University, he went to Harvard Medical School, where he earned degrees in medicine and public health. Today he is an associate professor of medicine at Harvard Medical School and the director of the Center for Cardiovascular Disease Prevention at Brigham and Women's Hospital in Boston.

In recent years, popular thinking among physicians held that the best predictor of potential heart attacks was the presence of high cholesterol in a patient's blood. But Ridker discovered that about half of all heart attacks occur in people with normal cholesterol levels. (In fact, my cholesterol levels were in the normal range before I had my heart attack.) Ridker determined to find out why.

Ridker began reviewing reports and other materials to try to identify the culprit. His research indicated that inflammation of the arteries might be responsible, so he began a large-scale study to begin gathering data for his theory. Physicians commonly thought that the kind of low level inflamation he desired to track couldn't be detected. "There were a lot of naysayers," says Ridker.[64]

GOING AGAINST THE FLOW

That didn't deter Ridker. He has always gone against the flow of popular thinking. As an undergraduate at Brown, for example, he didn't study pre-med like his fellow future doctors. He studied furniture design. He explains, "I knew for the rest of my life I would be learning biology and science, so I thought college should be used for other things."[65]

He discovered that a substance called C-reactive protein (CRP) is present in the blood of those with a high risk of heart attack. Tracking that substance is as reliable and inexpensive as checking cholesterol. And in fact, it better predicts heart problems than elevated LDL (the bad) cholesterol.

Heart disease is currently the number one killer of men and women in the U.S. Unfortunately, half of those who were strong candidates to die of heart attacks had no good way to find out. Ridker has helped to change all that. Because he questioned popular thinking and went in another direction, fewer people are likely to die of heart disease.

IT'S TIME TO BECOME UNPOPULAR

Economist John Maynard Keynes, whose ideas profoundly influenced economic theory and practices in the twentieth century, asserted, "The difficulty lies not so much in developing new ideas as in escaping from the old ones." Going against popular thinking can be difficult, whether you're a businessperson bucking company tradition, a pastor introducing new types of music to his church, a new mother rejecting old

> "The difficulty lies not so much in developing new ideas as in escaping from the old ones."
> —John Maynard Keynes

wives' tales handed down from her parents, or a teenager ignoring currently popular styles.

Many of the ideas in this book go against popular thinking. If you value popularity over good thinking, then you will severely limit your potential to learn the types of thinking encouraged by this book.

Popular thinking is . . .

- Too Average to Understand the Value of Good Thinking,
- Too Inflexible to Realize the Impact of Changed Thinking,
- Too Lazy to Master the Process of Intentional Thinking,
- Too Small to See the Wisdom of Big-picture Thinking,
- Too Satisfied to Unleash the Potential of Focused Thinking,
- Too Traditional to Discover the Joy of Creative Thinking,
- Too Naive to Recognize the Importance of Realistic Thinking,
- Too Undisciplined to Release the Power of Strategic Thinking,
- Too Limiting to Feel the Energy of Possibility Thinking,
- Too Trendy to Embrace the Lessons of Reflective Thinking,
- Too Shallow to Question the Acceptance of Popular Thinking,
- Too Proud to Encourage the Participation of Shared Thinking,

- Too Self-absorbed to Experience the Satisfaction of Unselfish Thinking, and
- Too Uncommitted to Enjoy the Return of Bottom-Line Thinking.

If you want to become a good thinker, then start preparing yourself for the possibility of becoming unpopular.

WHY YOU SHOULD QUESTION THE ACCEPTANCE OF POPULAR THINKING

I've given you some broad reasons for questioning the acceptance of popular thinking. Now allow me to be more specific:

1. Popular Thinking Sometimes Means Not Thinking

My friend Kevin Myers sums up the idea of popular thinking by saying, "The problem with popular thinking is that it doesn't require you to think at all." Good thinking is hard work. If it were easy, everybody would be a good thinker.

> "The problem with popular thinking is that it doesn't require you to think at all."
> —Kevin Myers

Unfortunately, many people try to live life the easy way. They don't want to do the hard work of thinking or pay the price of success. It's easier to do what other people do and hope that *they* thought it out.

Look at the stock market recommendations of some experts. By the time they publish their picks, most are following a trend, not creating one or even riding its crest. The people who are going to make money on the stocks they recommend have already done so by the time the general public hears about it.

When people blindly follow a trend, they're not doing their own thinking.

2. *Popular Thinking Offers False Hope*

Benno Muller-Hill, a professor in the University of Cologne genetics department, tells how one morning in high school he stood last in a line of forty students in the school yard. His physics teacher had set up a telescope so that his students could view a planet and its moons. The first student stepped up to the telescope. He looked through it, but when the teacher asked if he could see anything, the boy said no; his nearsightedness hampered his view. The teacher showed him how to adjust the focus, and the boy finally said he could see the planet and moons. One by one, the students stepped up to the telescope and saw what they were supposed to see. Finally, the second to last student looked into the telescope and announced that he could not see anything.

"You idiot," shouted the teacher, "you have to adjust the lenses."

The student tried, but he finally said, "I still can't see anything. It is all black."

The teacher, disgusted, looked through the telescope himself, and then looked up with a strange expression. The lens cap still covered the telescope. None of the students had been able to see anything![66]

Many people look for safety and security in popular thinking. They figure that if a lot of people are doing something, then it must be right. It must be a good idea. If most people accept it, then it probably represents fairness, equality, compassion, and sensitivity, right? Not necessarily.

Popular thinking said the earth was the center of the universe, yet Copernicus studied the stars and planets and proved mathematically that the earth and the other planets in our solar system revolved around the sun. Popular thinking said surgery didn't require clean instruments, yet Joseph Lister studied the high death rates in hospitals and introduced antiseptic practices that immediately saved lives. Popular thinking said that women shouldn't have the right to vote, yet people like Emmeline Pankhurst and Susan B. Anthony fought for and won that right. Popular thinking put the Nazis into power in Germany, yet Hitler's regime murdered millions and nearly destroyed Europe. We must always remember there is a huge difference between acceptance and intelligence. People may say that there's safety in numbers, but that's not always true.

Sometimes it's painfully obvious that popular thinking isn't good and right. Other times it's less evident. For example, consider the staggering number of people in the United States who have run up large amounts of debt on their credit cards. Anyone who is financially astute will tell you that's a bad idea. Yet millions follow right along with the popular thinking of buy now, pay later. And so they pay, and pay, and pay. Many promises of popular thinking ring hollow. Don't let them fool you.

3. Popular Thinking Is Slow to Embrace Change

Popular thinking loves the status quo. It puts its confidence in the idea of the moment, and holds on to it with all its might. As a result, it resists change and dampens innovation. Donald M. Nelson, former president of the Society of Independent Motion Picture Producers, criticized popular thinking when he asserted, "We must discard the idea that past

> "We must stop assuming that a thing which has never been done before probably cannot be done at all."
> —Donald M. Nelson

routine, past ways of doing things, are probably the best ways. On the contrary, we must assume that there is probably a better way to do almost everything. We must stop assuming that a thing which has never been done before probably cannot be done at all."

A few years ago I saw the movie *October Sky*. It's based on the true story of Homer Hickam, a boy who grew up in Coalwood, a company-owned coal mining town in West Virginia. Everyone in the town, except perhaps the best athletes, seemed destined to work in the mines, and few residents seemed willing to fight that common fate.

Homer, however, desired something different. Following the Soviet Union's launch of Sputnik, Homer wanted to build rockets and become an astronaut. He fought an uphill battle. Who wanted to embrace an idea that went against the popular thinking of the town? Certainly not Homer's own father, the superintendent of the town's mine, who wanted to see Homer follow in his footsteps.

Homer eventually fought his way out of Coalwood, received his education from Virginia Tech, and became an engineer at NASA, training astronauts. He has since retired and works as a consultant to NASA. But he still hasn't given up his dream of going into space. If you desire to fight popular thinking as Homer Hickam did, then realize that it may be a slow process—but a worthwhile one.

4. Popular Thinking Brings Only Average Results

The bottom line? Popular thinking brings mediocre results. Here is popular thinking in a nutshell:

Popular = Normal = Average

It's the least of the best and the best of the least. We limit our success when we adopt popular thinking. It represents putting in the least energy to just get by. You must reject common thinking if you want to accomplish uncommon results.

How to Question the Acceptance of Popular Thinking

Popular thinking has often proved to be wrong and limiting. Questioning it isn't necessarily hard, once you cultivate the habit of doing so. The difficulty is in getting started. Begin by doing the following things:

1. Think Before You Follow

Many individuals follow others almost automatically. Sometimes they do so because they desire to take the path of least resistance. Other times they fear rejection. Or they believe there's wisdom in doing what everyone else does. But if you want to succeed, you need to think about what's best, not what's popular.

Challenging popular thinking requires a willingness to be unpopular and go outside of the norm. Following the tragedy of September 11, 2001, for example, few people willingly chose to travel by plane. But that was the *best* time to travel: crowds were down, security was up, and airlines were cutting prices. About a month after the tragedy, my wife, Margaret, and I heard that Broadway shows had lots of seats and many New York hotel rooms remained empty. Popular thinking said, stay away from New York. We used that as an opportunity. We got cheap plane tickets to the city, booked a room in a great hotel for about half price, and got tickets to the most sought-after show: *The Producers.* As we took our seats in the theater, we sat next to a woman beside herself with excitement.

"I can't believe I'm finally here," she said to us. "I've waited so long. This is the *best* show on Broadway—and the hardest to get tickets to." Then she turned to look me in the eye and said, "I've had my tickets for a year and a half, waiting to see this show. How long ago did you get yours?"

"You won't like my answer," I replied.

"Oh, come on," she said. "How long?"

"I got mine five days ago," I answered. She looked at us in horror. By the way, she was right. It's one of the best shows we've seen in a while. And we got to see it only because we were willing to go against popular thinking when everyone else was staying at home.

As you begin to think against the grain of popular thinking, remind yourself that

- Unpopular thinking, even when resulting in success, is largely underrated, unrecognized, and misunderstood.
- Unpopular thinking contains the seeds of vision and opportunity.
- Unpopular thinking is required for all progress.

The next time you feel ready to conform to popular thinking on an issue, stop and think. You may not want to create change for its own sake, but you certainly don't want to blindly follow just because you haven't thought about what's best.

2. Appreciate Thinking Different from Your Own

One of the ways to embrace innovation and change is to learn to appreciate how others think. To do that, you must continually expose yourself to people different from yourself. My brother, Larry Maxwell—a good businessman and an innovative thinker—continually challenges popular thinking by thinking differently. He says,

Most of our people in sales and middle management come from businesses with products and services different from ours. That constantly exposes us to new ways of thinking. We also discourage our people from active participation in formal business and trade associations and fraternities because their thinking is quite common. They don't need to spend lots of time thinking the way everyone else in the industry does.

As you strive to challenge popular thinking, spend time with people with different backgrounds, education levels, professional experiences, personal interests, etc. You will think like the people with whom you spend the most time. If you spend time with people who think out of the box, you're more likely to challenge popular thinking and break new ground.

3. Continually Question Your Own Thinking

Let's face it, any time we find a way of thinking that works, one of our greatest temptations is to go back to it repeatedly, even if it no longer works well. The greatest enemy to tomorrow's success is sometimes today's success. My

> The greatest enemy to tomorrow's success is sometimes today's success.

friend Andy Stanley recently taught a leadership lesson at INJOY's Catalyst Conference called "Challenging the Process." He described how progress must be preceded by change, and he pointed out many of the dynamics involved in questioning popular thinking. In an organization, he said, we should remember that every tradition was originally a good idea—and perhaps even revolutionary. But every tradition may not be a good idea for the future.

In your organization, if you were involved in putting into

place what currently exists, then it's likely that you will resist change—even change for the better. That's why it's important to challenge your own thinking. If you're too attached to your own thinking and how everything is done now, then nothing will change for the better.

4. Try New Things in New Ways

When was the last time you did something for the first time? Do you avoid taking risks or trying new things? One of the best ways to get out of the rut of your own thinking is to innovate. You can do that

> When was the last time you did something for the first time?

in little, everyday ways: Drive to work a different way from normal. Order an unfamiliar dish at your favorite restaurant. Ask a different colleague to help you with a familiar project. Take yourself off of auto pilot.

Unpopular thinking asks questions and seeks options. In 1997, my three companies moved to Atlanta, Georgia. It's a great city, but traffic at peak times can get crazy. Immediately after moving here, I began looking for and testing alternate routes to desired destinations so that I would not be caught in traffic. From my house to the airport, for example, I have discovered and used nine routes within eight miles and twelve minutes from one another. Often I am amazed to see people sitting on the freeway when they could be moving forward on an alternate route. What is the problem? Too many people have not tried new things in new ways. It is true: most people are more satisfied with old problems than committed to finding new solutions.

How you go about doing new things in new ways is not as important as making sure you do it. (Besides, if you try to do new things in the same way that everyone else does, are you really going against popular thinking?) Get out there and do something different today.

> Most people are more satisfied with old problems than committed to finding new solutions.

5. Get Used to Being Uncomfortable

When it comes right down to it, popular thinking is comfortable. It's like an old recliner adjusted to all the owner's idiosyncrasies. The problem with most old recliners is that no one has *looked* at them lately. If so, they'd agree that it's time to get a new one!

If you want to reject popular thinking in order to embrace achievement, you'll have to get used to being uncomfortable. It's like swimming upstream. I know, because I've worked at it most of my life.

SWIMMING AGAINST THE
CURRENT OF POPULAR THINKING

Swimming against the current of popular thinking has been a good exercise for me, although it has been difficult. For years I coasted along with popular thinking because I was a people pleaser. In the world of churches, people love tradition; pastors, too. Often when I went along with what everyone else believed, however, down deep I knew I was not reaching my potential.

When I did find the courage to go against the flow, it allowed me to break new ground and reap good results. And it allowed me to help others. During the course of my career, I've continually fought popular thinking. Here are some of the issues I faced:

- Most people said going to seminary following college was the correct educational path for a pastor—I rejected that thinking and got the practical experience I needed first.

- Most people said counseling and administrative skills were the keys to success as a pastor—I rejected that thinking and worked on my leadership skills.

- Most people said I was too young to pastor the denomination's best church—I rejected that thinking and accepted the position of senior pastor at age 25.

- Most people said the doctrine of my church would hinder its growth—I rejected that thinking and in 1976, ours became the fastest growing church in Ohio.

- Most people said a large, paid staff was necessary to grow a large church—I rejected that thinking and we grew to more than 1,000 people with only two full-time pastors.

- Most people said leadership cannot be taught—I rejected that thinking, and I began writing *Developing the Leader Within You* so that I could teach others to lead.

- Most people said it was unwise to leave my denomination—I rejected that thinking, and today I recognize that it has allowed me to reach many more people.

- Most people said it would be "career suicide" to follow the founding pastor of a church—I rejected that thinking and not only did the church grow, but today, twenty-two years later, that pastor and I are good friends.

- Most people said the church could not be relocated because of zoning challenges—I rejected that thinking, and fifteen years later, the church has relocated.

- Most people said that if I resigned as the church's senior pastor, the church would falter—I rejected that thinking, and today the church is bigger than when I led it.

- Most people said that leaving the pastorate would diminish my effectiveness with pastors—I rejected that thinking, and today I serve more pastors than ever.

- Most people said that it would be almost impossible for me to teach leadership in the business world and still reach the religious world—I rejected that thinking, and today I am doing both and having a ball.

My early years of swimming against the current of popular thinking were the most difficult for me. I lacked experience and didn't have the confidence of a few wins under my belt. My unpopular thinking and decisions often made *me* unpopular and kept me from being "one of the boys." Today it is much easier to swim against the current. (It's amazing what a few accomplishments can do for a person's self-image and confidence.) One of my greatest challenges today is to keep people around me who will think differently and express those differences to me. Thankfully, I have people who do exactly that.

If you reject popular thinking and make decisions based upon what works best and what is right rather than what is commonly accepted, know this: in your early years you won't be as wrong as people think you are. In your later years, you won't be as right as people think you are. And all through the years, you will be better than you thought you could be.

THINKING QUESTION

Am I consciously rejecting the limitations of common thinking in order to accomplish uncommon results?

Putting Unpopular Thinking into Action

1. Appreciate how other people think by getting into the head of an innovative thinker. Go to the bookstore or get on Amazon.com and browse biographies. Pick a book written about someone you ordinarily would not relate to or be attracted to. If you love numbers and facts, read about an artist. If you're artistic, read a business biography. If you avoid politics, read about a politician. You get the idea. Take your mind where it doesn't ordinarily go, and try to appreciate the thinking of the subject of the biography.

2. Increase your ability to feel uncomfortable. Do something every day in a way different from what you're used to. Drive to the office or grocery store a different way every day this week. Arrange your day in an order different from how you usually do. Go on a different kind of date with your partner. Go to a concert featuring music different from what you generally like. Shake up your mind!

3. We all have things in our lives that are overdue for change—ideas, processes, or objects that were great and revolutionary when new but need to be changed now. Find something of that nature and change it. If you're having trouble finding something in need of change, ask friends, a colleague, or your spouse to help you.

Skill 9

Encourage the Participation of Shared Thinking

"None of us is as smart as all of us."
—KEN BLANCHARD

What Were They Thinking?

"I desire what is good. Therefore, everyone who doesn't agree with me is a traitor."
—KING GEORGE III OF ENGLAND

In early 2002, I was invited to meet and spend time with one of the greatest basketball coaches of all time; Pat Summit of the University of Tennessee. I love basketball. I started playing the game when I was ten years old. I played all four years in high school and was recruited to play college ball. It was my passion while growing up. So of course I felt excited when I learned that I could meet Summit. Who wouldn't? She's received more honors than any other coach, except John Wooden! Consider a sampling of what she has achieved:

- Winner of 6 NCAA Titles (1987, 1989, 1991, 1996, 1997, 1998)
- Winner of 20 SEC Championships
- Coached a perfect season in 1997-98 (39-0)
- Inducted into the Basketball Hall of Fame (2000)
- Inducted into the Women's Basketball Hall of Fame (1999)
- Named Naismith Women's Collegiate Coach of the Century (Wooden was the men's honoree)
- Winner of the John Bunn Award (1990)
- Her Lady Vols named ESPN Team of the Decade (1990s)
- Past Lady Vols players include 11 Olympians, 16 Kodak All-Americans, 53 All-SEC Players, and 25 professionals
- Coached Women's U.S. Olympic team to first gold medal (1984)
- Youngest coach to reach 300 victories (at age 37)
- One of 17 college coaches to have won 700 or more games
- Too many "Coach of the Year" honors to list

I received the invitation to visit Knoxville because the manager of the Lady Volunteers basketball team, April Ford, knew me through the leadership training I had done for her mother, Karen Ford (whom you met in Chapter 2). Pat Summit had also evidently read some of my books, so she invited me to be a "guest coach."

I knew I was in for a great experience. First, I had the chance to spend a few minutes with Pat in her office, talking about leadership and teamwork. One of the best things she told me regarded recruiting. She said that each year, of the thousand players who come out of high school to play college ball, only eight or nine have what it takes to bring a team a national championship. Every year her goal is to recruit one of those players. Obviously, she has succeeded often.

After Pat and I talked, I got to speak to the team before its game with Old Dominion. Then, during the game, I sat right behind the bench where I could listen in to what she and the team discussed. At halftime, I got to go into the locker room with her and the team.

A number of things struck me about Pat. First, she's very warm, but extremely intense. She's known for her competitiveness. She says that comes, in part, from having a demanding father and three very competitive older brothers. A quote from her book, *Reach for the Summit,* tells you everything you need to know about her desire to win: "I have never had a losing season, at anything. In every basketball season I have participated in, I ended up with a winning record."[67]

Second, she's a leader through and through. You can see it in how she runs the team, how she interacts with her assistant coaches, how she motivates and teaches her players. She's very strategic in her communication with each player. She watches them and carefully listens to them to make sure they're tracking with her before she coaches them. Too many coaches, she says, try to give instruction to their players when no foundation of understanding has been established.

But I'll tell you the thing that struck me the most about her. Even given her strong personality and leadership ability, she chooses to practice shared thinking. Let me give you an example. During halftime, she stays away at first from her players. Instead, she has the players interact by themselves and do their own review and diagnosis of the game. They share their observations and solutions without any coach's input. (She's very strategic about cultivating this ability. She engages a psychologist to teach her players how to interact productively without the involvement of coaches.) While the players talk, Pat meets with her coaches to hear their observations. After about ten minutes, everyone gets together. The players review their findings and tentative adjustments for Pat, and she and the other coaches make any needed corrections to their plans. It's a model of shared thinking.

You can also see how Pat employs shared thinking when she calls a timeout. In the first fifteen seconds, she doesn't even look at her players. She's too busy receiving thoughts from her assistant coaches. When she finally talks to the players, she accepts input from them, too. Pat recalls that during a game against Vanderbilt, while she talked with her assistants, Chamique Holdsclaw—only a freshman at the time—tugged on Pat's sleeve and interrupted her. "Give me the ball," she said. "Give me the *ball*." Pat gave her the ball, Holdsclaw scored, and the team won.[68]

WHY YOU SHOULD ENCOURAGE THE PARTICIPATION OF SHARED THINKING

Good thinkers, especially those who are also good leaders, understand the power of shared thinking. They know that when they value the thoughts and ideas of others, they receive the compounding results of shared thinking and accomplish more than they ever could on their own. Pat Summit not only practices the participation of shared thinking with her team, she is teaching the young women who play for her how to do it, too.

Those who participate in shared thinking understand the following:

1. Shared Thinking Is Faster than Solo Thinking

We live in a truly fast-paced world. To function at its current rate of speed, we can't go it alone. I think the generation of young men and women just entering the workforce sense that very strongly. Perhaps that is why they value community so highly and are more likely to work for a company they like than one that pays them well. Working with others is like giving yourself a shortcut.

If you want to learn a new skill quickly, how do you do it? Do you go off by yourself and figure it out, or do you get someone to show you how? You can always learn more quickly from someone with experience—whether you're trying to learn how to use a new software package, develop your golf swing, or cook a new dish.

2. Shared Thinking Is More Innovative than Solo Thinking

We tend to think of great thinkers and innovators as soloists, but the truth is that the greatest innovative thinking doesn't occur in a vacuum. Innovation results from collaboration. Albert Einstein once remarked, "Many times a day I realize how much my own outer and inner life is built upon the labors of my fellow men, both living and dead, and how earnestly I must exert myself in order to give in return as much as I have received."

> We tend to think of great thinkers and innovators as soloists, but the truth is that the greatest innovative thinking doesn't occur in a vacuum.

Shared thinking leads to greater innovation, whether you look at the work of researchers Marie and Pierre Curie, surrealists Luis Brunel and Salvador Dali, or songwriters John Lennon and Paul McCartney. If you combine your thoughts with the thoughts of others, you will come up with thoughts you've never had!

3. Shared Thinking Brings More Maturity than Solo Thinking

As much as we would like to think that we know it all, each of us is probably painfully aware of our blind spots and areas of

> If you combine the thoughts you have and the thoughts that others have, you will come up with thoughts you've never had!

inexperience. When I first started out as a pastor, I had dreams and energy, but little experience. To try to overcome that, I attempted to get several high-profile pastors of growing churches to share their thinking with me. In the early 1970s, I wrote letters to the ten most successful pastors in the country, offering them what was a huge amount of money to me at the time ($100) to meet me for an hour, so that I could ask them questions. When one said yes, I'd visit him. I didn't talk much, except to ask a few questions. I wasn't there to impress anyone or satisfy my ego. I was there to learn. I listened to everything he said, took careful notes, and absorbed everything I could. Those experiences changed my life.

You've had experiences I haven't, and I've had experiences you haven't. Put us together and we bring a broader range of personal history—and therefore maturity—to the table. If you don't have the experience you need, hook up with someone who does.

4. Shared Thinking Is Stronger than Solo Thinking

Philosopher-poet Johann Wolfgang von Goethe said, "To accept good advice is but to increase one's own ability." Two heads are

> "To accept good advice is but to increase one's own ability."
> —Johann Wolfgang von Goethe

better than one—when they are thinking in the same direction. It's like harnessing two horses to pull a wagon. They are stronger pulling together than either is individually. But did you know that when they pull together, they can move more weight than the sum of what they can move individually? A synergy comes from working together. That same kind of energy comes into play when people think together.

5. Shared Thinking Returns Greater Value than Solo Thinking

Because shared thinking is stronger than solo thinking, it's obvious that it yields a higher return. That happens because of the compounding action of shared thinking. But it also offers other benefits. The personal return you receive from shared thinking and experiences can be great. Clarence Francis sums up the benefits in the following observation: "I sincerely believe that the word relationships is the key to the prospect of a decent world. It seems abundantly clear that every problem you will have—in your family, in your work, in our nation, or in this world—is essentially a matter of relationships, of interdependence."

6. Shared Thinking Is the Only Way to Have Great Thinking

I believe that every great idea begins with three or four good ideas. And most good ideas come from shared thinking. Play-

> "He that is taught only by himself has a fool for a master."
> —Ben Jonson

wright Ben Jonson said, "He that is taught only by himself has a fool for a master."

When I was in school, teachers put the emphasis on being right and on doing better than the other students, rarely on working together to come up with good answers. Yet all the answers improve when they make the best use of everyone's thinking. If we each have one thought, and together we have two thoughts, then we always have the potential for a great thought.

HOW TO ENCOURAGE THE
PARTICIPATION OF SHARED THINKING

Some people naturally participate in shared thinking. Any time they see a problem, they think, *Who do I know who can help with this?* Leaders tend to be that way. So do extroverts. However, you don't have to be either of those to benefit from shared thinking. Use the following steps to help you improve your ability to harness shared thinking:

1. Value the Ideas of Others

First, believe that the ideas of other people have value. If you don't, your hands will be tied. How do you know if you truly want input from others? Ask yourself these questions:

- *Am I emotionally secure?* People who lack confidence and worry about their status, position, or power tend to reject the ideas of others, protect their turf, and keep people at bay. It takes a secure person to consider others' ideas. Years ago, an emotionally insecure person took a key position on my board of directors. After a couple of meetings, it became obvious to the other board members that this individual would not positively contribute to the organization. I asked a seasoned leader on the board, "Why does this person always do and say things that hinder our progress?" I'll never forget his reply: "Hurting people hurt people."
- *Do I place value on people?* You won't value the ideas of a

person if you don't value and respect the person himself. Have you ever considered your conduct around people you value, versus those you don't? Look at the differences:

If I Value People	If I Don't Value People
I want to spend time with them	I don't want to be around them
I listen to them	I neglect to listen
I want to help them	I don't offer them help
I am influenced by them	I ignore them
I respect them	I am indifferent

- *Do I value the interactive process?* A wonderful synergy often occurs as the result of shared thinking. It can take you places you've never been. Publisher Malcolm Forbes asserted, "Listening to advice often accomplishes far more than heeding it." I must say, I didn't always value shared thinking. For many years, I tended to withdraw when I wanted to develop ideas. Only reluctantly did I work on ideas with others. When a colleague challenged me on this, I started to analyze my hesitancy. I realized that it went back to my college experience. Some days in the classroom I could tell that a teacher was unprepared to lecture and instead spent the class time asking us to give our uninformed opinions on a subject. Most of the time, the opinions seemed no better than mine. I had come to class so that the professor could teach me. I realized that the process of sharing ideas wasn't the problem; it was *who* was doing the talking. Shared thinking is only as good as the people doing the sharing. Since learning that lesson, I have embraced the interactive process, and now I believe it is one of my strengths. Still, I always think about whom I bring around the table for a shared thinking session. (I'll tell you my guidelines for whom I invite later in this chapter.)

You must open yourself up to the *idea* of sharing ideas before you will engage in the *process* of shared thinking.

2. Move from Competition to Cooperation

Jeffrey J. Fox, author of *How to Become CEO,* says, "Always be on the lookout for ideas. Be completely indiscriminate as to the source. Get ideas from customers, children, competitors, other industries, or cab drivers. It doesn't matter who thought of an idea."[69]

> "Always be on the lookout for ideas. Be completely indiscriminate as to the source. . . . It doesn't matter who thought of an idea."
> —Jeffrey J. Fox

A person who values cooperation desires to complete the ideas of others, not compete with them. If someone asks you to share ideas, focus on helping the team, not getting ahead personally. And if you are the one who brings people together to share their thoughts, praise the idea more than the source of the idea. If the best idea always wins (rather than the person who offered it), then all will share their thoughts with greater enthusiasm.

3. Have an Agenda When You Meet

I enjoy spending time with certain people, whether we discuss ideas or not: my wife, Margaret; my children; my grandchildren; my parents. Though we often do discuss ideas, it doesn't bother me if we don't; we are family. When I spend time with nearly anyone else in my life, however, I have an agenda. I know what I want to accomplish.

The more I respect the wisdom of the person, the more I listen. For example, when I meet with someone I'm mentoring, I let the person ask the questions, but I expect to do most of the talking. When I meet with someone who mentors me, like Bill Bright, I mostly keep my mouth shut. In other relationships, the give and take is more even. But no matter with whom I meet, I have a reason for getting together and I have an expectation for what I'll give to it and get from it. That's true whether it's for business or pleasure.

4. Get the Right People Around the Table

The greatest secret to winning shared thinking is having the right people around the table. Remember Pat Summit and the Lady Vols? At the end of halftime, Pat asked all of her coaches whether they had anything to add. Then she turned to me and said, "Do

> The greatest secret to winning shared thinking is having the right people around the table.

you have anything to share?" In that moment, I knew she was being nice to her "guest coach," but I knew I had nothing of value to add. I was totally out of my league. Pat didn't call me into the circle during timeouts in the second half of the game, either. Why? Because I had nothing to contribute. Blessed is he who knows when to keep his mouth shut!

To get anything of value out of shared thinking, you need to have people around the table who bring something *to* the table. As you prepare to ask people to participate in shared thinking, use the following criteria for the selection process. Choose . . .

- People whose greatest desire is the success of the ideas.
- People who can add value to another's thoughts.

- People who can emotionally handle quick changes in the conversation.
- People who appreciate the strengths of others in areas where they are weak.
- People who understand their place of value at the table.
- People who place what is best for the team before themselves.
- People who can bring out the best thinking in the people around them.
- People who possess maturity, experience, and success in the issue under discussion.
- People who will take ownership and responsibility for decisions.
- People who will leave the table with a "we" attitude, not a "me" attitude.

Too often we choose our brainstorming partners based on feelings of friendship or circumstances or convenience. But that doesn't help us to discover and create the ideas of the highest order. Who we invite to the table makes all the difference.

5. Compensate Good Thinkers and Collaborators Well

Successful organizations practice shared thinking. If you lead an organization, department, or team, then you can't afford to be without people who are good at shared thinking. As you recruit and hire, look for good thinkers who value others, have experience with the collaborative process, and are emotionally secure. Then pay them well and challenge them to use their thinking skills and share their ideas often. Nothing adds value like a lot of good thinkers putting their minds together.

TEAM EFFORT

No matter what you're trying to accomplish, you can do it better with shared thinking. That is why I spend much of my life teaching leadership. Good leadership helps to put together the right people at the right time for the right purpose so that everybody wins. I'm such a strong believer in shared thinking that I engage in that process even when writing a book.

Most people think that books are the brain children of a single mind. Some-

> No matter what you're trying to accomplish, you can do it better with shared thinking.

times that's true, especially among fiction writers and poets (although Stephen King, possibly the most popular novelist of our time, attributes much of his success to his wife). But like anything else, a book is better when it is the project of shared thinking.

When I began working on this book, I spent a lot of time in reflective thinking to figure out how I think and to consider the thinking habits of successful people. Then I developed an outline of the book. It wasn't long before I engaged other good thinkers in the process. Early on, I kicked ideas around with my writer, Charlie Wetzel. I also got feedback from my publisher, Rolf Zettersten. During these early stages we identified the title of the book.

Once we landed on the title and basic outline, I assembled a team of good, creative thinkers to brainstorm more ideas for the book. That group included

- Dick Biggs
- Kevin Donaldson
- Linda Eggers
- Tim Elmore

- John Hull
- Gabe Lyons
- Larry Maxwell
- Kevin Myers
- Dan Reiland
- Kevin Small
- J. L. Smith
- Dave Sutherland
- Charlie Wetzel
- Kathie Wheat

Some of these people I consulted individually, but I brought the majority of them into a room for a wonderful time of synergistic thinking. Then Kathie Wheat, my research assistant, started pulling together story ideas and information. And as Charlie and I finished chapters, his wife, Stephanie, and my wife, Margaret, read them and gave their valuable feedback, helping us discover things we missed. And a few chapters, I sent to individuals who are particularly good at a specific kind of thinking.

Could I have written this book by myself? Certainly. Is it better now because I asked people to help me? Definitely! My friends and colleagues make me better than I am alone. The same thing can happen for you. All it takes is the right people and a willingness to participate in shared thinking.

THINKING QUESTION

Am I consistently including the heads of others to think "over my head" and achieve compounding results?

Putting Shared Thinking into Action

1. How well do you practice shared thinking? Are you naturally likely or unlikely to include others in the thinking process when you face a difficult challenge or troublesome problem? Rate yourself on a scale of 1 to 10, with 1 indicating that you *never* include others and a 10 indicating that you nearly *always* invite others to share their ideas. Write your score here: _____

If you gave yourself anything lower than a seven, then you need to do some soul searching. Indicate why you feel reluctant to include others in the process:

    ____ I don't place a high value on people
    ____ I don't value the interactive thinking process
    ____ I am not a very secure person
    ____ Other:

Pursue changes that will help you address this issue.

2. If you don't already have one, create a list of good thinkers and their areas of expertise. Then the next time you have a worthwhile problem to solve or task to tackle, look over your list and bring together people who can add value, according to the criteria given in the chapter on who should be brought to the table.

Thinker	Expertise
_____	_____
_____	_____
_____	_____
_____	_____
_____	_____

3. Review your calendar for the coming week. Examine every appointment or activity you have listed and think about the agenda for each. Take some time to clarify what you want to get out of an interaction with each person (or what you expect to give to him or her). Write down questions or ideas in your planner or on an index card, if necessary. Then when you meet, make sure to touch on your agenda items. Afterward, jot down any ideas that may come. You may be surprised by how much more productive your time will become.

Skill 10

Experience the Satisfaction of Unselfish Thinking

*"We cannot hold a torch to light another's path
without brightening our own."*
—BEN SWEETLAND

What Were They Thinking?

*"If it is true that we are here to help others,
then what exactly are the OTHERS here for?"*
—AUTHOR UNKNOWN

So far in this book, we've discussed many kinds of thinking that can help you to achieve more. Each of them has the potential to make you more successful. Now I want to acquaint you with a kind of thinking with the potential to change your life in another way. It might even redefine how you view success. Let me start by telling you a story.

THE LONG ROAD OF SUCCESS

In 1885, a young man named George used every penny he had to travel to Highland, Kansas. He felt excited over his admission to Highland College, for getting an education had always been his driving goal. As a youngster, he and his brother had walked nine miles each way to school in order to start their education. At age twelve, he had left home for good to attend high school, supporting himself doing chores and housework similar to what he'd done at home on the farm. At age twenty, he was ready to start college. When he got to Highland College, however, his hopes where dashed. Even though his application had been accepted, school officials turned him away when they discovered that he was black.

For a few years after that, George tried to establish a homestead. He had a knack for growing things, but his desire to continue his education drew him back to his goal. In 1890, he once again attempted to enroll in school. This time he was accepted by Simpson College, which accepted students regardless of race. He opened a laundry to support himself and studied painting and piano.

By all accounts, George excelled in the arts. One of his works won first prize at the 1893 World's Fair in Chicago. He wrote poetry and saw it published in newspapers. He had musical talent. In 1891 when he transferred to Iowa State College, he continued working in the arts, but also pursued other interests. He became a trainer for the school's athletic teams. He joined the campus' military regiment, where he rose to the group's highest rank—captain. And he led the YMCA and the debate club.

But George also underwent another change while at Iowa State. He changed his major from art to agriculture. Why would he do such a thing, especially when he loved art so much?

James Wilson, formerly the dean of Agriculture at Iowa State, recalled the reason in this statement addressed to George:

> I remember when I first met you, you said you wanted to get an agricultural education so you could help your race. I had never known anything more beautiful than that said by a student. I know the taste you have for painting and the success you have made along that line, and I said, 'Why not push your studies along that line to some extent?' When you replied that that would be of no value to your colored brethren, that also was magnificent.[70]

George summed up the change in his studies simply by saying, art "would not do [my] people as much good."[71]

George Washington Carver went on to receive his degree in agriculture from Iowa State. His excellence in the fields of botany and horticulture prompted two professors to encourage him to stay on as a graduate student and earn his master's degree. He did. And in the process, he worked as the assistant botanist for the College Experiment Station, developed expertise in plant pathology and mycology, and became the first African American faculty member at Iowa State College.

THE NEXT STEP

In April of 1896, Carver received an unusual offer from Dr. Booker T. Washington of the Tuskegee Institute. Would he take a teaching position there and become the school's director of Agriculture? Washington said,

> I cannot offer you money, position, or fame. The first two you have. The last from the position you now occupy you

will no doubt achieve. These things I now ask you to give up. I offer you in their place: work . . . hard, hard work, the task of bringing a people from degradation, poverty, and waste to full manhood. Your department exists only on paper and your laboratory will have to be in your head."[72]

Carver could have lived a comfortable life in Iowa. He was respected professionally, an accepted member of the community, and had built relationships there. Yet all of these things he now gave up to move to Alabama, in the heart of the deep South where he would be regarded as a second-class citizen. He did it because he practiced unselfish thinking and wanted to help people in more difficult circumstances than himself.

While at Tuskegee Institute, Carver earned the respect of such innovators as Thomas Edison and Henry Ford, as well as that of several presidents of the United States. His agricultural research and discoveries improved farming throughout the country, and he was especially successful at helping poor, black farmers of the South. His development of an extension program to take the classroom out to the people made a real difference in the lives of thousands. And he accomplished all that he did with minimal resources or support.

If Carver had focused his attention on patenting his findings or building a business on his discoveries, as Thomas Edison and Henry Ford had done, he could have become a very rich man. But that was never his goal. He spent his whole life focused on unselfish thinking, trying to help others. Carver explained his philosophy this way: "It is not the style of clothes one wears, neither the kind of automobile one drives, nor the amount of money one has in the bank, that counts. These mean

> George Washington Carver found more than success. By thinking beyond himself, he discovered significance.

nothing. It is simply service that measures success." George Washington Carver found more than success. By thinking beyond himself, he discovered significance.

WHY YOU SHOULD STRIVE FOR THE SATISFACTION OF UNSELFISH THINKING

Unselfish thinking can often deliver a return greater than any other kind of thinking. Take a look at some of its benefits:

1. Unselfish Thinking Brings Personal Fulfillment

Few things in life bring greater personal rewards than helping others. Charles H. Burr believed, "Getters generally don't get happiness; givers get it."

Helping people brings great satisfaction. When you spend your day unselfishly serving others, at night you can lay down

> "There is no more noble occupation in the world than to assist another human being—to help someone succeed."
> —Alan Loy McGinnis

your head with no regrets and sleep soundly. In *Bringing Out the Best in People*, Alan Loy McGinnis remarked, "There is no more noble occupation in the world than to assist another human being—to help someone succeed."

Even if you have spent much of your life pursuing selfish gain, it's never too late to have a change of heart. Even the most miserable person, like Charles Dickens' Scrooge, can turn his life around and make a difference for others. That's what Alfred Nobel did. When he saw his own obituary in the newspaper (his brother had died and the editor had written about the wrong Nobel, saying that the explosives his company produced had killed many people), Nobel vowed to promote peace and acknowledge contributions to humanity. That is how the Nobel Prizes came into being.

2. Unselfish Thinking Adds Value to Others

In 1904, Bessie Anderson Stanley wrote the following definition of success in *Brown Book Magazine*:

> He has achieved success who has lived well, laughed often and loved much; who has enjoyed the trust of pure women, the respect of intelligent men and the love of little children, who has filled his niche and accomplished his task; who has left the world better than he found it, whether by an improved poppy, a perfect poem, or a rescued soul; who has never lacked appreciation of earth's beauty or failed to express it, who has always looked for the best in others and given them the best he had, whose life was an inspiration, whose memory a benediction.

When you get outside of yourself and make a contribution to others, you really begin to live.

3. Unselfish Thinking Encourages Other Virtues

When you see a four-year-old, you expect to observe selfishness. But when you see it in a forty-year-old, it's not very attractive, is it?

Of all the qualities a person can pursue, unselfish thinking seems to make the biggest difference toward cultivating other virtues. I think that's because the ability to give unselfishly is so difficult. It goes against the grain of human nature. But if you can learn to think unselfishly and become a giver, then it becomes easier to develop many other virtues: gratitude, love, respect, patience, discipline, etc.

4. Unselfish Thinking Increases Quality of Life

The spirit of generosity created by unselfish thinking gives people an appreciation for life and an understanding of its higher values. Seeing those in need and giving to meet that need puts a lot of things into perspective. It increases the quality of life of the giver and the receiver. That's why I believe that

> There is no life as empty as the self-centered life. There is no life as centered as the self-empty life.

> There is no life as empty as the self-centered life.
> There is no life as centered as the self-empty life.

If you want to improve your world, then focus your attention on helping others.

5. Unselfish Thinking Makes You Part of Something Greater than Yourself

Merck and Company, the global pharmaceutical corporation, has always seen itself as doing more than just producing products and making a profit. It desires to serve humanity. In the mid 1980s, the company developed a drug to cure river blindness, a disease that infects and causes blindness in millions of people, particularly in developing countries. While it was a good product, potential customers couldn't afford to buy it. So what did Merck do? It developed the drug anyway, and in 1987 announced that it would give the medicine free to anyone who needed it. As of 1998, the company had given more than 250 million tablets away.[73]

George W. Merck says, "We try never to forget that medicine is for the people. It is not for the profits. The profits follow, and if we have remembered that, they have never failed to appear." The lesson to be learned? Simple. Instead of trying to be great, be part of something greater than yourself.

6. Unselfish Thinking Creates a Legacy

Jack Balousek, president and chief operating officer of True North Communications, says, "Learn, earn, return—these are the three phases of life. The first third should be devoted to education, the second third to building a career and making a living, and the last third to giving back to others—returning something in gratitude. Each state seems to be a preparation for the next one."

> "Learn, earn, return—these are the three phases of life."
> —Jack Balousek

If you are successful, it becomes possible for you to leave an inheritance *for* others. But if you desire to do more, to create a legacy, then you need to leave that *in* others. When you think unselfishly and invest in others, you gain the opportunity to create a legacy that will outlive you.

HOW TO EXPERIENCE THE SATISFACTION OF UNSELFISH THINKING

I think most people recognize the value of unselfish thinking, and most would even agree that it's an ability they would like to develop. Many people, however, are at a loss concerning how to change their thinking. To begin cultivating the ability to think unselfishly, I recommend that you do the following:

1. Put Others First

The process begins with realizing that everything is not about you! That requires humility and a shift in focus. In *The Power of Ethical Management,* Ken Blanchard and Norman Vincent Peale wrote, "People with humility don't think less of themselves; they just think of themselves less."

If you want to become less selfish in your thinking, then you need to stop thinking about your wants and begin focusing on others' needs. Paul the Apostle exhorted, "Do nothing out of selfish ambition or vain conceit, but in humility consider others better than yourselves. Each of you should look not only to your own interests, but also to the interests of others."[74] Make a mental and emotional commitment to look out for the interests of others.

> "People with humility don't think less of themselves; they just think of themselves less."
> —Ken Blanchard and Norman Vincent Peale

2. Expose Yourself to Situations Where People Have Needs

It's one thing to believe you are willing to give unselfishly. It's another to actually do it. To make the transition, you need to put yourself in a position where you can see people's needs and do something about it. Once you do, follow the advice of Tod Barnhart, author of *The Five Rituals of Wealth.* One of his five rituals says, "Act with impact—you've got to give to live!" Here is his advice:

> Give to everyone who asks. I firmly believe that our purpose in life is to try to make a difference in the lives of those around us. . . . I give something—no matter how

small—to everyone who asks me. . . . It's fun, especially if you don't do it out of obligation. Believe me, it will change the way you think about yourself and about your money."[75]

The kind of giving you do isn't important at first. You can serve at your church, make donations to a food bank, volunteer professional services, or give to a charitable organization. The point is to learn how to give and to cultivate the habit of thinking like a giver.

3. Give Quietly or Anonymously

Once you have learned to give of yourself, then the next step is to learn to give when you cannot receive anything in return. It's almost always easier to give when you receive recognition for it than it is when no one is likely to know about it. The people who give in order to receive a lot of fanfare, however, have already received any reward they will get. There are spiritual, mental, and emotional benefits that come only to those who give anonymously. If you've never done it before, try it.

I have some friends who "adopt" a family for Christmas every year. They visit a caring agency to pick the family, often a single parent who would otherwise be unable to afford Christmas. My friends and their children plan the Christmas meal, buy gifts, and make certain that the family's Christmas is special. Then the agency delivers the goodies so that my friends can remain anonymous. The one thing my friends ask for is a picture of the family so that they can pray for them. (I found out about their practice because I asked about the picture on their refrigerator.) My friends say this activity is often the highlight of Christmas for their family.

4. Invest in People Intentionally

The highest level of unselfish thinking comes when you give of yourself to another person for their personal development or well-being. If you're married or a parent, you know this from personal experience. What does your spouse value most highly: money in the bank or your time freely given? What would small children really rather have from you: a toy or your undivided attention? The people who love you would rather have you than what you can give them.

If you want to become the kind of person who invests in people, then consider others and their journey so that you can collaborate with them. Each relationship is like a partnership created for mutual benefit. As you go into any relationship, think about how you can invest in the other person so that it becomes a win-win situation. Here is how relationships most often play out:

I win, you lose—I win only once.
You win, I lose—You win only once.
We both win—We win many times.
We both lose—Goodbye, partnership!

The best relationships are win-win. Why don't more people go into relationships with that attitude? I'll tell you why: most people want to make sure that they win first. Unselfish thinkers, on the other hand, go into a relationship and make sure that the other person wins first. And that makes all the difference.

My life changed in 1975 when I read a book by Zig Zigler titled *See You at the Top.* In it I found the following words, the catalyst that encouraged me to learn unselfish thinking: "If you will help others achieve what they want, they will help you achieve what you want."

I immediately embraced that principle and began to practice

unselfish thinking. In fact, I founded three companies out of my desire to invest in other people. I started INJOY to help pastors learn how to lead more effectively. INJOY Stewardship Services began when a businessman asked me to help his church raise money to build an auditorium. EQUIP was birthed out of my desire to raise up one million leaders internationally. Little did I realize that my desire to add value to others would be the thing that added value to me!

> Little did I realize that my desire to add value to others would be the thing that added value to me!

5. *Continually Check Your Motives*

François de la Rochefoucauld said, "What seems to be generosity is often no more than disguised ambition, which overlooks a small interest in order to secure a great one." The hardest thing for most people is fighting their natural tendency to put themselves first. That's why it's important to continually examine your motives to make sure you're not sliding backwards into selfishness.

Do you want to check your motives? Then follow the modeling of Benjamin Franklin. Every day, he asked himself two questions. When he got up in the morning, he would ask, "What good am I going to do today?" And before he went to bed, he would ask, "What good have I done today?" If you can answer those questions with selflessness and integrity, you can keep yourself on track.

GIVE WHILE YOU LIVE

In the fall of 2001, we all witnessed a demonstration of unselfish thinking unlike anything we had seen in the United

States for many years. Who can forget September 11? I had just finished teaching a leadership lesson when my assistant, Linda Eggers, came into the studio to announce the tragic news. Like most Americans, I remained riveted to the television all day and heard the reports of the firefighters and police officers who raced into the World Trade Center towers to help others, never worrying about their own safety.

In the days following the tragedy, millions of Americans expressed a great desire to do something that would help the situation. I had the same desire. INJOY was scheduled to do a training via simulcast on September 15, the Saturday following the tragedy. Our leadership team decided to add a one and a half hour program titled "America Prays" to the end of the simulcast. In it, my friend Max Lucado wrote and read a prayer, expressing the heart's cry of millions. Franklin Graham prayed for our national leaders. Jim and Shirley Dobson gave advice to parents on how to help their children deal with the event. And Bruce Wilkinson and I asked the simulcast viewers to give financially to the people injured on September 11. Amazingly, they gave $5.9 million, which World Vision graciously agreed to distribute to those in need. Unselfish thinking and giving turned a very dark hour into one of light and hope.

Less than two weeks after the tragedy, I was able to travel to Ground Zero in New York City. I went to view the site of the destruction, to thank the men and women clearing away the wreckage, and to pray for them. I can't really do justice to what I saw. I've traveled to New York dozens of times. It's one of my favorite places in the world. My wife and I had been up in the towers with our children many times before and have wonderful memories of that area. To look at the place where the buildings had once stood and to see nothing but rubble, dust, and twisted metal—it's simply indescribable.

What many Americans didn't realize is that for many months

people worked diligently to clean up the site. Many were New York City firefighters and other city workers. Others were volunteers. They worked around the clock, seven days a week. And when they came across the remains of someone in the rubble, they called for silence and reverently carry them out.

Since I am a clergyman, I was asked to wear a clerical collar upon entering the area. As I walked around, many workers saw the collar and asked me to pray for them. It was a humbling privilege.

American educator Horace Mann said, "Be ashamed to die until you have won some victory for humanity." According to this standard, New York City's firefighters are certainly prepared for death. The service they perform is often truly heroic. You

> "Be ashamed to die until you have won some victory for humanity."
> —Horace Mann

and I may never be required to lay down our lives for others, as they did. But, we can give to others in different ways. We can be unselfish thinkers who put others first and add value to their lives. We can work with them so that they go farther than they thought possible.

THINKING QUESTION

Am I continually considering others and their journey in order to think with maximum collaboration?

PUTTING UNSELFISH THINKING INTO ACTION

1. Do you want to help yourself put others first and to develop and maintain unselfish motives? Then set unselfish goals for

yourself. Think about some things you could do to help others that will in no way benefit you (other than to give you internal satisfaction). Set an amount of money to give away this year (anonymously, if possible). Decide on a number of hours a week or month to serve others. Find a ministry or cause that you will help to succeed—not necessarily by trying to run it, but by assisting wherever you are asked to. It will help you to begin thinking more unselfishly if you set goals and look for ways to meet them. How will you help?

_____

_____

2. Many times the most rewarding acts of unselfishness come when people obey an inner sense to meet another's need. During the coming week, tune your intuitive radar to look for human needs. When you perceive a need and feel prompted to help, follow through on that inclination. If you *really* want to become a better unselfish thinker, try to look for needs continually for a prolonged period of time (like a year).

3. An investment in a person ultimately pays the highest return because it can result in changed lives. Think about what you have to invest in another person. What skills do you possess that someone would benefit from learning? What life experiences have you had that can help another person? What resources do you possess that ought to be shared?

_____

_____

_____

Once you have figured out what you have to give, then look for someone with need and potential who would be glad to receive it, and invest in that person.

4. The next time you put together a deal or develop a professional relationship, think in terms of win-win. If both you and the other person would not benefit, then don't go through with the deal. And once you've determined that it will be good for both of you, make the effort to guarantee that the other person wins first.

Skill 11

Enjoy the Return of Bottom-Line Thinking

"There ain't no rules around here. We're trying to accomplish something."
—THOMAS EDISON, INVENTOR

What Were They Thinking?

"A bus station is where a bus stops. A train station is where a train stops. On my desk, I have a workstation . . ."
—AUTHOR UNKNOWN

How do you figure out the bottom line for your organization, business, department, team, or group? In many businesses, the bottom line is literally the bottom line. Profit determines whether you are succeeding. But dollars should not always be the primary measure of success. Would you measure the ultimate success of your family by how much money you had at the end of the month or year? And if you run a non-profit or volunteer organization, how would you know whether you were performing at your highest potential? How do you think bottom line in that situation?

A NON-PROFIT'S BOTTOM LINE

Frances Hesselbein had to ask herself exactly that question in 1976, when she became the national executive director of the Girl Scouts of America. When she first got involved with the Girl Scouts, running the organization was the last thing she expected. She and her husband, John, were partners in Hesselbein Studios, a small family business that filmed television commercials and promotional films. She wrote the scripts and he made the films. In the early 1950s, she was recruited as a volunteer troop leader at the Second Presbyterian Church in Johnstown, Pennsylvania. Even that was unusual, since she had a son and no daughters. But she agreed to do it on a temporary basis. She must have loved it, because she led the troop for nine years!

In time, she became council president and a member of the national board. Then she served as executive director of the Talus Rock Girl Scout Council, a full-time paid position. By the time she took the job as CEO of the national organization, the Girl Scouts was in trouble. The organization lacked direction, teenage girls were losing interest in scouting, and it was becoming increasingly difficult to recruit adult volunteers, especially with greater numbers of women entering the workforce. Meanwhile, the Boy Scouts was considering opening itself to girls. Hesselbein desperately needed to bring the organization back to the bottom line.

"We kept asking ourselves very simple questions," she says. "What is our business? Who is our customer? And what does the customer consider value? If you're the Girl Scouts, IBM, or AT&T, you have to manage for a mission."[76] Hessel-

> "If you're the Girl Scouts, IBM, or AT&T, you have to manage for a mission."
> —Frances Hesselbein

bein's focus on mission enabled her to identify the Girl Scouts' bottom line. "We really are here for one reason: to help a girl reach her highest potential. More than any one thing, that made the difference. Because when you are clear about your mission, corporate goals and operating objectives flow from it."[77]

Once she figured out her bottom line, she was able to create a strategy to try to achieve it. She started by reorganizing the national staff. Then she created a planning system to be used by each of the 350 regional councils. And she introduced management training to the organization.

Hesselbein didn't restrict herself to changes in leadership and organization. In the 1960s and '70s, the country had changed and so had its girls—but the Girl Scouts hadn't. Hesselbein tackled that issue, too. The organization made its activities more relevant to the current culture, giving greater opportunities for use of computers, for example, rather than hosting a party. She also sought out minority participation, created bilingual materials, and reached out to low income households. If helping girls reach their highest potential was the group's bottom line, then why not be more aggressive helping girls who traditionally have fewer opportunities? The strategy worked beautifully. Minority participation in the Girl Scouts tripled.

In 1990, Hesselbein left the Girl Scouts after making it a first-class organization. She went on to become the founding president and CEO of the Peter F. Drucker Foundation for Nonprofit Management, and now serves as chairman of its board of governors. And in 1998, she was awarded the Presidential Medal of Freedom. President Clinton said of Hesselbein during the ceremony at the White House, "She has shared her remarkable recipe for inclusion and excellence with countless organizations whose bottom line is measured not in dollars, but in changed lives."[78] He couldn't have said it better!

WHY YOU SHOULD ENJOY THE
RETURN OF BOTTOM-LINE THINKING

If you're accustomed to thinking of the bottom line only as it relates to financial matters, then you may be missing some things crucial to you and your organization. Instead, think of the bottom line as the end, the take away, the desired result. Every activity has its own unique bottom line. If you have a job, your work has a bottom line. If you serve in your church, your activity has a bottom line. So does your effort as a parent, or spouse, if you are one.

> Think of the bottom line as the end, the take away, the desired result.

As you explore the concept of bottom-line thinking, recognize that it can help you in many ways:

1. Bottom-Line Thinking Provides Great Clarity

What's the difference between bowling and work? When bowling, it takes only three seconds to know how you've done! That's one reason people love sports so much. There's no waiting and no guessing about the outcome.

Bottom-line thinking makes it possible for you to measure outcomes more quickly and easily.

> Bottom-line thinking makes it possible for you to measure outcomes more quickly and easily.

It gives you a benchmark by which to measure activity. It can be used as a focused way of ensuring that all your little activities are purposeful and line up to achieve a larger goal.

2. Bottom-Line Thinking Helps You Assess Every Situation

When you know your bottom line, it becomes much easier to know how you're doing in any given area. When Frances Hesselbein began running the Girl Scouts, for example, she measured everything against the organization's goal of helping a girl reach her highest potential—from the organization's management structure (which she changed from a hierarchy to a hub) down to what badges the girls could earn. There's no better measurement tool than the bottom line.

3. Bottom-Line Thinking Helps You Make the Best Decisions

Decisions become much easier when you know your bottom line. When the Girl Scouts were struggling in the 1970s, outside organizations tried to convince its members to become women's rights activists or door-to-door canvassers. But under Hesselbein, it became easy for the Girl Scouts to say no. It knew its bottom line, and it wanted to pursue its goals with focus and fervency.

4. Bottom-Line Thinking Generates High Morale

When you know the bottom line and you go after it, you greatly increase your odds of winning. And nothing generates high morale like winning. How do you describe sports teams that win the championship, or company divisions that achieve their goals, or volunteers who achieve their mission? They're excited. Hitting the target feels exhilarating. And you can hit it only if you know what it is.

5. Bottom-Line Thinking Ensures Your Future

If you want to be successful tomorrow, you need to think bottom line today. That's what Frances Hesselbein did, and she turned the Girl

> If you want to be successful tomorrow, you need to think bottom line today.

243

Scouts around. Look at any successful, lasting company, and you'll find leaders who know their bottom line. They make their decisions, allocate their resources, hire their people, and structure their organization to achieve that bottom line.

How to Enjoy the Return of Bottom-Line Thinking

It isn't hard to see the value of the bottom line. Most people would agree that bottom-line thinking has a high return. But learning how to be a bottom-line thinker can be challenging.

1. Identify the Real Bottom Line

The process of bottom-line thinking begins with knowing what you're really going after. It can be as lofty as the big-picture vision, mission, or purpose of an organizaion. Or it can be as focused as what you want to accomplish on a particular project. What's important is that you be as specific as possible. If your goal is for something as vague as "success," you will have a painfully difficult time trying to harness bottom-line thinking to achieve it.

The first step is to set aside your "wants." Get to the results you're really looking for, the true essence of the goal. Set aside any emotions that may cloud your judgment and remove any politics that may influence your perception. What are you really trying to achieve? When you strip away all the things that don't really matter, what are you compelled to achieve? What must occur? What is acceptable? That is the real bottom line.

Recently, I went through this process of bottom-line thinking with the board of directors of EQUIP. For the past seven years, EQUIP has given leadership training to three groups: college students, urban church pastors, and national church leaders overseas. Though all three areas were seeing success, I sensed that our divided focus was preventing us from reaching our potential in any of the three areas. That meant we needed to make a decision, and to do that, we had to figure out our bottom line.

We asked ourselves this question: "If we could accomplish only one thing in the lifetime of EQUIP, what would it be?" We discussed the issue and prayed about it, and we came to the conclusion that we *had* to teach leadership internationally. For us, that is what *must* occur. That was our bottom line.

Our vision is to raise up and train one million leaders internationally by 2007. For months since our decision to refocus, we have mapped out a strategy that will enable us to reach this goal. The result is an increase in ideas, energy, dollars, and partnerships with others. Why? Because we identified and embraced the bottom line.

2. *Make the Bottom Line the Point*

Have you ever been in a conversation with someone whose intentions seem other than stated? Sometimes the situation reflects intentional deception. But it can also occur when the person doesn't know his own bottom line.

The same thing happens in companies. Sometimes, for example, an idealistically stated mission and the real bottom line don't jibe. Purpose and profits compete. Earlier, I quoted George W. Merck, who stated, "We try never to forget that medicine is for the people. It is not for the profits. The profits follow, and if we have remembered that, they have never failed to appear." He probably made that statement to remind those in his organization that profits *serve* purpose—they don't compete with it.

245

If making a profit were the real bottom line, and helping people merely provided the means for achieving it, then the company would suffer. Its attention would be divided, and it would neither help people as well as it could nor make as much profit as it desired.

3. Create a Strategic Plan to Achieve the Bottom Line

Bottom-line thinking achieves results. Therefore, it naturally follows that any plans that flow out of such thinking must tie directly to the bottom line—and there can be only one, not two or three. Once

| Bottom-line thinking achieves results. |

the bottom line has been determined, a strategy must be created to achieve it. In organizations, that often means identifying the core elements or functions that must operate properly to achieve the bottom line. This is the leader's responsibility.

I've already introduced you to Dave Sutherland, the president of one of my companies, ISS. The bottom line of ISS is helping churches raise $1 billion a year to build facilities, helping them extend their potential reach. Dave is an outstanding strategic thinker, but he is also an incredible bottom-line thinker. He has determined that to achieve its bottom line, ISS needs three core elements:

- *Marketing:* Its objective is to contact churches who need to raise money and get them to let one of the company's representatives present to the church's board what ISS can do for them. The bottom-line goal: the number of board presentation appointments made.

- *Field Sales:* Its job is to meet with the church's pastor and board, find out their needs, explain how ISS can help them, and invite them to let ISS partner with them. The bottom-line goal: the number of agreements made with churches.

- *Consulting:* Its job is to provide customized on-site consulting to the churches so that they raise the money they desire. The bottom-line goal: client satisfaction.

Any objective can be broken down in a similar way. The important thing is that when the bottom line of each activity is achieved, then THE bottom line is achieved. If the sum of the smaller goals doesn't add up to the real bottom line, then either your strategy is flawed or you've not identified your real bottom line.

4. Align Team Members with the Bottom Line

Once you have your strategy in place, make sure your people line up with your strategy. Ideally, all team members should know the big goal, as well as their individual role in achieving it. They need to know their personal bottom line and how that works to achieve the organization's bottom line.

5. Stick with One System and Monitor Results Continually

Dave Sutherland believes that some organizations get into trouble by trying to mix systems. He maintains that many kinds of systems can be successful, but mixing different systems or continually changing from one to another leads to failure. Dave says,

Bottom-line thinking cannot be a one-time thing. It has to be built into the system of working and relating and achieving. You can't just tune into the desired result every now and then. Achieving with bottom-line thinking must be a way of life, or it will send conflicting messages. I am a bottom-line thinker. It is a part of my "system" for achievement. I practice it every day. No other measurements—no wasted efforts.

> "Achieving with bottom-line thinking must be a way of life, or it will send conflicting messages."
> —Dave Sutherland

Dave calls members of his field team every night to ask the bottom-line question they expect to hear. He continually keeps his eye on the company's bottom line by monitoring it for every core area.

Kevin Small, the president of INJOY, practices a similar discipline. Since January of 2002, he began holding a daily flash meeting with everyone who represents a key area of the company. In thirty minutes, they review the numbers from the previous day and measure those numbers against their goals and projections for the year. They also review their top priorities for the day and state how they relate to the bottom line. Kevin says it has made a huge difference:

> We are well ahead of our forecasts because we are watching the numbers. We're managing more efficiently, and so far we're having a good year. That's happening because we're continually aware of the bottom line. I can tell you where we're in trouble. I can tell you where we are not. You can ask me anything about the business, and I can tell you about it right now. If we didn't do this, I wouldn't have known that we had a problem with our subscription programs this week. I wouldn't have been able to tell you that we needed to hire another person for customer service.

My bottom line has gone from a thirty-day cycle to a daily cycle. So I've gone from thinking about the bottom line once a month to every single morning. And soon we will be able to do it in real time. This makes me a much better leader. Our founder, John Maxwell, teaches about the Law of Navigation in *The 21 Irrefutable Laws of Leadership.* That law says that anyone can steer the ship, but it takes a leader to chart the course. Daily, I chart the course with my team and we make mid-course corrections. We know where we are and where we want to go.

Kevin is a natural leader. He's young and still developing, but he's getting better every day, because he desires to learn and grow. He is constantly on the lookout for opportunities, but he also keeps his eye on the bottom line.

THE BOTTOM LINE ON THE BOTTOM LINE

When it comes right down to it, regardless of your bottom line, you can improve it with good thinking. And bottom-line thinking has a great return because it helps to turn your ideas into results. Like no other kind of mental processing, it can help you to reap the full potential of your thinking and achieve whatever you desire.

THINKING QUESTION

Am I staying focused on the bottom line so that I can gain the maximum return and reap the full potential of my thinking?

Putting Bottom-Line Thinking into Action

1. How much have you thought about your own bottom line? Do you know why you're doing what you're doing in your career? Have you figured out what you're trying to accomplish in your family life? If someone asked, would you be able to tell him for what purpose you've been put on this earth?

Your life can be more fulfilling and your thinking can be more fruitful if you know your purpose. Give some thought to each of the following areas. Then try to write succinctly your bottom line for each.

Career: _____

Marriage: _____

Parenting: _____

Recreation: _____

Service/Ministry: _____

Life Purpose: _____

Don't feel bad if you don't have perfect clarity on all of these issues. It takes most people years to figure it all out. This exercise is merely a starting point.

2. Chose a major goal in your life or career. Write the goal here:

_____

_____

A. Now, set aside a block of time this week to determine the bottom line for this goal. Remember to make sure that the bottom line is the point, not a substitute for another unstated goal or just a step toward it. Once you've figured out what the bottom line is, write it here.

B. Your next step is to develop a strategy for accomplishing the bottom line. What are the core elements required to achieve it? What are the major objectives? Break it down to its most fundamental parts.

C. Now determine what kind of help will be required to achieve the goal. Can you do it alone? Will it require the aid of friends or colleagues? Will you need to start your own organization to do it? Is there an organization that already exists that you can join to accomplish it?

D. Your next step is to align the people with the strategy for achieving the bottom line. (If your goal requires the help of others, and you have little experience leading people, you will want to begin a personal growth plan for leadership development.)

E. Figure out how you will monitor your progress and that of the others involved. Remember, you will be able to achieve the bottom line only if you continually keep your eye on it.

AFTERTHOUGHT

You never know where good thinking might take you. In the spring of 1999, David Phillips saw an offer by the Healthy Choice food company. It would give 500 airline miles for every barcode a consumer sent in to the company by the end of the year. And the company would double the miles if it received the proof of purchase by May 31. Most of us wouldn't have given that tidbit a second thought. But it got David Phillips *thinking*. He had been looking for a cheap way to get his family to Europe for a vacation, and this seemed like a great opportunity.

Phillips scoured discount grocery stores for the least expensive Healthy Choice product he could find, and it turned out to be chocolate pudding. Phillips, an engineer, did some quick calculating and then started buying all the pudding he could find. He cleaned out every location of a discount grocery chain in his town. In the end, he bought more than *12,500* cups of pudding!

Next, Phillips faced the challenge of getting the lids with the bar codes off of the pudding cups by the deadline, only a couple of weeks away. He and his family worked on them for a while, but too slowly. So he employed creative thinking and came up with a solution. He donated the pudding to the Salvation Army. Their volunteers removed and returned the lids, and the people they served would get the pudding as part of their meals. On top of that, Phillips would receive a tax deduction!

When all was said and done, Phillips earned more than 1.2 million frequent flyer miles. For an investment of $3,140, he received enough miles to take his family to Europe—not once, but more than *thirty* times. And because he topped the one million mile mark, he became a member of American Airlines AAdvantage Gold Club for life.[79]

Phillips wasted no time using his miles for travel. In the first year, he took his wife and daughters to Italy, Spain, and London for Easter, to Sweden for Christmas, and to Cancun for Thanksgiving (along with three other family members). And you can bet that if he hasn't used all his miles by the time they are ready to expire, he will employ good thinking to come up with a way to make use of them.

OUR JOURNEY TOGETHER

David Phillips' story shows that good thinking can make an impact on any area of life. I hope you have enjoyed our journey together through the kinds of thinking that make people successful. And I hope you have learned more about yourself and how you think. Your thinking, more than anything else, shapes the way you live. It's really true that if you change your thinking, you can change your life.

Take a moment to evaluate yourself in each area of thinking discussed in the book. Rate yourself on a scale of 1 to 10 (with 10 being the highest):

_____ *Understand the Value of Good Thinking:* Do I believe that good thinking can change my life?
_____ *Realize the Impact of Changed Thinking:* Is my desire for success and to improve my life strong enough to prompt me to change my thinking?

_____ *Master the Process of Intentional Thinking:* Am I willing to pay the price to cultivate the habit of giving birth to, nurturing, and developing great thoughts every day?

_____ *Acquire the Wisdom of Big-Picture Thinking:* Am I thinking beyond myself and my world so that I process ideas with a holistic perspective?

_____ *Unleash the Potential of Focused Thinking:* Am I dedicated to removing distractions and mental clutter so that I can concentrate with clarity on the real issue?

_____ *Discover the Joy of Creative Thinking:* Am I working to break out of my "box" of limitations so that I explore ideas and options that will enable me to experience creative breakthroughs?

_____ *Recognize the Importance of Realistic Thinking:* Am I building a solid mental foundation on facts so that I can think with certainty?

_____ *Release the Power of Strategic Thinking:* Am I implementing strategic plans that give me direction for today and increase my potential for tomorrow?

_____ *Feel the Energy of Possibility Thinking:* Am I unleashing the enthusiasm of possibility thinking to find solutions even for situations that seem impossible?

_____ *Embrace the Lessons of Reflective Thinking:* Am I regularly revisiting the past to gain a true perspective and think with understanding?

_____ *Question the Acceptance of Popular Thinking:* Am I consciously rejecting the limitations of common thinking in order to achieve uncommon results?

_____ *Encourage the Participation of Shared Thinking:* Am I consistently including the heads of others to think "over my head" and attain compounding results?

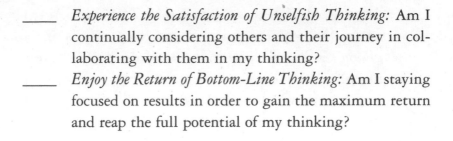

_____ *Experience the Satisfaction of Unselfish Thinking:* Am I continually considering others and their journey in collaborating with them in my thinking?

_____ *Enjoy the Return of Bottom-Line Thinking:* Am I staying focused on results in order to gain the maximum return and reap the full potential of my thinking?

I trust that your thinking has improved. However, the reality is that nobody can expect to master every kind of thinking. That's why I want to offer you this advice. On each kind of thinking, if you score . . .

8–10 Spend 80% of your time doing this type of thinking.

6–7 Spend 20% of your time doing this type of thinking.

0–5 Bring someone onto your team who scores an 8, 9, or 10 for this type of thinking.

In the opening chapter, I described how my father decided to change the way he thought when he was a young man. Recently, my wife, Margaret, and I went to a banquet honoring my father, sponsored by the organization to which my father belonged for fifty-five years. We sat with my parents at their table, and we talked about his decision to dedicate his life to thinking the way successful people did. That decision enabled my parents to rear three children who are committed to adding value to others. It was the catalyst that set my father apart from many of his contemporaries and helped him to rise to leadership positions within the organization. It allowed him and Mom to enjoy more than 60 years of marriage together.

I reflected on these things as I listened to the banquet's speaker describe the contributions of my father's life, and it brought me to tears. When the crowd stood as my dad went to the stage, I stood with them, cheering the loudest, because I knew him the best. And I thought, *There is a man who changed his thinking, and it changed his life—and the lives of others, including me.*

The same thing can happen for you. That is why I wrote this book. May thinking become your greatest tool for creating the world you desire.

NOTES

1. John C. Maxwell, *Think on These Things* (Kansas City, Missouri: Beacon Hill, 1979), 13.

2. Philippians 4:8 (NRSV).

3. David J. Schwartz, *The Magic of Thinking Big* (New York: Fireside, 1959), 66.

4. James Allen, *The Wisdom of James Allen* (San Diego: Laurel Creek Press, 1997), 31.

5. James Allen, *The Wisdom of James Allen* (San Diego: Laurel Creek Press, 1997), 54.

6. See Proverbs 23:7.

7. "Wal-Mart Stores, Inc. at a Glance," www.walmartstores.com, January 29, 2002.

8. Source unknown.

9. James C. Collins and Jerry I. Porras, *Built to Last: Successful Habits of Visionary Companies* (New York: Harper Business, 1994), 213.

10. The American Covenant.

11. John C. Maxwell, *The Winning Attitude* (Nashville: Thomas Nelson, 1991), 24.

12. Martin J. Grunder Jr., *The 9 Super Simple Steps to Entrepreneurial Success* (Dayton, Ohio: Gatekeeper Books, 2002), 96.

13. Guy Gilchrist, "Keeper of the Keys," *Mudpie* (Canton, Connecticut: Gilchrist Publishing, 2001). Used by permission.

14. J. J. O'Connor and E. F. Robertson, "Eratosthenes of Cyrene," www.history.mcs.st-andrews.ac.uk, January 28, 2002.

15. James C. Collins and Jerry I. Porras, *Built to Last: Successful Habits of Visionary Companies* (New York: Harper Business, 1994), 43-44.

16. John C. Maxwell, *Failing Forward: Turning Mistakes into Stepping Stones for Success* (Nashville: Thomas Nelson, 2000), 140.

17. "Crayola Trivia," www.crayola.com/mediacenter, March 6, 2002.

18. "Crayola Trivia," www.crayola.com/mediacenter, March 6, 2002.

19. "Crayola Trivia," www.crayola.com/mediacenter, March 6, 2002.

20. "The History and Development of Crayons," www.crayola.com/mediacenter, March 6, 2002.

21. Annette Moser-Wellman, *The Five Faces of Genius* (New York: Viking Press, 2001), 111.

22. "Coleco," Jones Telecommunications and Multimedia Encyclopedia, www.digitalcentury.com, March 14, 2002.

23. Al Ries, *Focus: The Future of Your Company Depends on It* (New York: Harper Business, 1996), 1.

24. M. Scott Peck, *The Road Less Traveled* (New York: Simon and Schuster, 1978), 27-28.

25. Jim Collins, "Good to Great," *Fast Company*, October 2001.

26. Joshua S. Rubinstein, David E. Meyer, and Jeffrey E. Evans, "Executive Control of Cognitive Processes in Task Switching," *Journal of Experimental Psychology,* quoted in *Leadership Strategies*, Volume 4, Number 12, December 2001.

27. "Martin First Female to Play, Score in Division I," www.espn.com, August 31, 2002.

28. "Female Giving Up Football," *The Atlanta Journal-Constitution*, January 21, 2002, E10.

29. Annette Moser-Wellman, *The Five Faces of Genius: The Skills to Master Ideas at Work* (New York: Viking, 2001), 6.

30. Skipp Ross with Carole C. Carlson, *Say Yes to Your Potential* (Nashville: Word, 1983).

31. Annette Moser-Wellman, *The Five Faces of Genius: The Skills to Master Ideas at Work* (New York: Viking, 2001), 9.

32. Ernie J. Zelinski, *The Joy of Not Knowing It All: Profiting from Creativity at Work or Play* (Chicago: VIP Books, 1994), 7.

33. Source unknown.

34. Michael Craig, "Priscilla Presley's Control of the Elvis Presley Estate," *The 50 Best (and Worst) Business Deals of All Time* (Franklin Lakes, New Jersey: Career Press, 2000), 18-22.

35. Cheryl Dahle, "Mind Games," *Fast Company*, January-February 2000, 170.

36. James Allen, *The Wisdom of James Allen* (San Diego: Laurel Creek Press, 1997).

37. "O'Leary Resigns as Notre Dame Football Coach," www.nd.edu, December 14, 2001.

38. Chris Palochko, "Security a Huge Issue at Super Bowl," sports.yahoo.com/nfl/news, February 2, 2002.

39. "Strategy" in *Webster's New World Dictionary of American English*, Third Collegiate Edition (Cleveland: Webster's New World, 1991).

40. Terry Ryan, *The Contest Winner of Defiance, Ohio: How My Mother Raised 10 Kids on 25 Words or Less* (New York: Touchstone, 2001), 25.

41. Terry Ryan, *The Contest Winner of Defiance, Ohio: How My Mother Raised 10 Kids on 25 Words or Less* (New York: Touchstone, 2001), 92.

42. Bobb Biehl, *Masterplanning: A Complete Guide for Building a Strategic Plan for Your Business, Church, or Organization* (Nashville: Broadman and Holman, 1997), 10.

43. Alan Axelrod, *Patton on Leadership: Strategic Lessons for Corporate Warfare* (Englewood Cliffs, New Jersey: Prentice Hall, 1999), 68.

44. "George S. Patton, Jr.," http://gi.grolier.com/wwii, May 28, 2002.

45. Janet Frankston, "Maxwell House Tie to Passover Spans Years," *The Atlanta Journal-Constitution*, March 27, 2002, F1.

46. Janet Frankston, "Maxwell House Tie to Passover Spans Years," *The Atlanta Journal-Constitution*, March 27, 2002, F10.

47. Sally Kline (editor), *George Lucas: Interviews* (Jackson: University Press of Mississippi, 1999), 32.

48. Thomas G. Smith, *Industrial Light & Magic: The Art of Special Effects* (New York: Ballantine Books, 1986), 10.

49. Bruce Handy, "The Force Is Back," *Time*, February 10, 1997, www.time.com.

50. Sally Kline (editor), *George Lucas: Interviews* (Jackson: University Press of Mississippi, 1999), 161.

51. Chris Salewicz, *George Lucas* (New York: Thunders' Mouth Press, 1998), 104.

52. Chris Salewicz, *George Lucas* (New York: Thunders' Mouth Press, 1998), 105.

53. Richard Corliss, "Ready, Set, Glow!" *Time*, April 26, 1999, www.time.com.

54. Chris Salewicz, *George Lucas* (New York: Thunders' Mouth Press, 1998), 113.

55. Jeremy M. Brosowsky, "No Payne, No Gayne: The Ins-and-Outs of Winning a Modern Olympic Bid, Courtesy of the Man Behind Atlanta's 1996 Plan, *Washington Business Forward*, August 2000, www.bizforward.com.

56. Eric Pooley, "Mayor of the World," *Time* December 31, 2001, www.time.com.

57. Sally Kline (editor), *George Lucas: Interviews* (Jackson: University Press of Mississippi, 1999), 96.

58. Sally Kline (editor), *George Lucas: Interviews* (Jackson: University Press of Mississippi, 1999), 121.

59. Joel Barker, *Future Edge* (New York: William Morrow & Co, 1992), 89.

60. "Leadership Lessons: An Interview with Don Soderquist," Willow Creek Association.

61. Author Unknown.

62. Mark Twain, *Following the Equator* (Hopewell, New Jersey: Ecco Press, 1996), 96.

63. "Chronology of Dr. Martin Luther King, Jr.," www.thekingcenter.com, January 3, 2002.

64. Alice Park, "Heart Mender," *Time*, August 20, 2001, 36.

65. Alice Park, "Heart Mender," *Time*, August 20, 2001, 36.

66. Benno Muller-Hill, "Science, Truth, and Other Values," *Quarterly Review of Biology*, Volume 68, Number 3 (September 1993), 399-407.

67. Pat Summit with Sally Jenkins, *Reach for the Summit* (New York: Broadway Books, 1998), 258.

68. Pat Summit with Sally Jenkins, *Reach for the Summit* (New York: Broadway Books, 1998), 69.

69. Jeffrey J. Fox, *How to Become CEO* (New York: Hyperion, 1998), 115.

70. Peter Duncan Burchard, "George Washington Carver in Iowa: Preparation for life serving humanity," The Gazette (Cedar Rapids, Iowa), www.gazetteonline.com, February 14, 1999.

71. "George Washington Carver," web.mit.edu/invent, April 27, 2002.

72. "George Washington Carver," www.biography.com, February 23, 2002.

73. "Mectizan Program Removes Darkness from an Ancient Disease," Corporate Philanthropy Report, Merck, p. 11, www.merck.com, April 27, 2002.

74. Philippians 2:3-4 (NIV).

75. Tod Barnhart, *The Five Rituals of Wealth: Proven Strategies for Turning the Little You Have into More Than Enough* (New York: Harperbusiness, 1996).

76. John A. Byrne, "Profiting from the Non-profits," *Business-Week*, March 26, 1990, 70.

77. John A. Byrne, "Profiting from the Non-profits," *Business-Week*, March 26, 1990, 72.

78. "Hesselbein Wins Presidential Medal of Freedom," www.drucker.org, December 19, 2001.

79. Kathleen Holder, "Engineer Finds Sweet Travel Deal in Cups of Pudding," www-dateline.ucdavis.edu, February 4, 2000.

We invite you to visit our companion web site at www. thinkingforachange.com. It has been designed to enhance and complete your learning experience. There you can take a FREE interactive assessment developed by the INJOY Group. It will help you to evaluate the strengths and weaknesses of your thinking skills. You will also find recommendations for how you can further your personal and professional development.

CHANGE YOUR THINKING AND CHANGE YOUR LIFE...

IMPROVE YOUR LEADERSHIP AND IMPACT THE LIVES OF OTHERS.

JOHN C. MAXWELL'S RECOMMENDATION FOR YOUR LEADERSHIP GROWTH:

STEP 1 Assess Your Leadership Strengths

You can take your leadership to the next level, and the INJOY Group will help you every step of the way! Begin your own leadership challenge at www.ThinkingforaChange.com. The 21 Laws leadership assessment will tell you where you are as a leader today and will guide you to where you need to be tomorrow.

Visit www.ThinkingforaChange.com and take your FREE assessment!

STEP 2 Begin Your Leadership Training

Log on to www.ThinkingforaChange.com and receive a free copy of *Leadership Aptitudes*. This lesson was specifically chosen from John C. Maxwell's Maximum Impact Club series to help you take the next step in your leadership training! *Leadership Aptitudes* is available to you either online in streaming audio format or, if you would prefer to add this lesson to your personal leadership training library, we can ship you a copy on

Visit www.ThinkingforaChange.com and download your FREE audio lesson! Available online or on audiocassette/CD.

either audiocassette or CD for a minimal shipping charge of $2.00.

STEP 3 Train with the Best Resources

If you're going to be the best, you've got to train with the best! Purchase the complete audio (for your personal use) and video (for group training) *21 Laws* series and maximize your leadership potential!

Living the 21 Irrefutable Laws of Leadership
Audio Curriculum by John C. Maxwell

You will achieve more than you ever imagined by simply listening to one leadership lesson, reading one chapter, and completing one assignment each month. With *Living the 21 Laws,* you'll have a leadership growth tool that will allow you to:

- **Evaluate your leadership strengths**
- **Create a proactive plan to improve your leadership skills**
- **Understand the laws so that you can readily teach them**

Learning the 21 Irrefutable Laws of Leadership
Video Curriculum by John C. Maxwell

How do you propel your organization to a new level? Make sure that you are all growing together! These dynamic videos will allow you to bring your entire leadership team together to develop a shared vision, a corporate purpose, and a unified effort. Plus, it will make teaching easier and less time-consuming for you.

STEP 4 Train with a Proven Coach

Let John C. Maxwell mentor you monthly!

Maximum Impact®: The Monthly Mentoring Leadership Club for Marketplace Leaders
Audio Program
(Available on CD or Audiocassette)

Most leaders will agree that regardless of how long they've been in a leadership position, there are issues they face every day where they would like some insight and helpful perspective. John will provide you with such mentorship on a monthly basis.

Learn about these resources at www.ThinkingforaChange.com.